SKILLS FOR DIRECT PRACTICE IN SOCIAL WORK

RUTH R. MIDDLEMAN
AND GALE GOLDBERG WOOD

Skills for Direct Practice
in Social Work

COLUMBIA UNIVERSITY PRESS

NEW YORK

Columbia University Press
New York   Chichester, West Sussex
Copyright © 1990 Columbia University Press
All rights reserved

Library of Congress Cataloging-in-Publication Data

Middleman, Ruth R.
Skills for direct practice in social work / Ruth R. Middleman and
Gale Goldberg Wood.
p.   cm.
Includes bibliographical references.
ISBN 0–231–05508–0
ISBN 0–231–05509–9 (pbk.)
1. Social service. 2. Social service—United States.
3. Social workers. 4. Social workers—United States.
I. Wood, Gale Goldberg.
II. Title.
HV40.M5168   1990
361.3′2′0973—dc20
89–71321
CIP

*Casebound editions of Columbia University Press books are printed on
permanent and durable acid-free paper.*

Printed in the United States of America

c 10 9 8 7 6 5 4 3 2 1
p 10

To the social worker who wants to know how to

Contents

PART IV: STRATEGIC SKILLS

Preface

We have been deliberate and serious people-watchers for many years. One of us collected samples of work through nonverbal interaction for twenty years before writing a book on the subject,[1] and this was in days when only three other authors published anything using "nonverbal" in the title.[2] That research is contained in just two sections of one chapter of the present work.[3]

Later, both of us explored the area of nonverbal communication in our doctoral dissertations,[4] and other writings,[5] and we used what we learned from our research to enrich our approach to social work practice. As we refined and sharpened our knowledge out of years of teaching Social Work Practice classes and Interactional Skills classes, we shared many of our insights and formulations with colleagues through workshops and presentations at professional conferences. Gradually, we devoted our attention to the specifics of worker behavior and skills.[6]

In *Social Service Delivery: A Structural Approach to Social Work Practice*,[7] we dealt with twenty-seven skills. Eleven skills are described and illustrated in *The Structural Approach to Direct Practice in Social Work*.[8] In this volume the reader will find those skills and many others that our subsequent study yielded—63 in all. We have included here skills for work with individuals and with both talking and non-talking groups.

We see these sixty-three identified skills as basic to facilitating the work with both individuals and groups. Of course, there may be other behaviors that could be identified. The range of specialized acts that animate particular techniques within specific theoretical approaches could extend our collection toward dictionary proportions and, we think, reap diminishing returns—a too-muchness, an information overload. These skills are generic to many theoretical approaches. While we see them in the context of the structural approach, they fit with the aims of diverse practice orientations in social work and other related professions.

Even though they may seem obvious or commonplace, we note here some of the cautions relevant to the skills we describe in this volume.

- In all work with others, one should pay attention to one's *persona,* i.e. to the overall impression one wishes to make. One aims to be unobtrusive, but there. This involves consideration of how one looks, one's clothes, jewelry, and the rest. The objective is to fit in rather than overwhelm by one's physical appearance.

- The words used with clients should not be pretentious. Vocabulary is crucial. The worker needs to understand several "languages," however: common everyday language and street language, scientific and technical language of social work and other disciplines or professions.

- When working with groups, one must get comfortable with practice-in-public. That is, in the group situation, others see and hear all that the social worker says and does. This demands a new kind of accountability and openness.

- Above all, one must work to cultivate *sensitivity*—to nuance, to difference, to the unknown and to the never-before experienced.

- And one must be able to say, "I don't know." If anything, such an admission will humanize the social worker to the other, and this is a most desirable state.

SKILLS FOR DIRECT PRACTICE IN SOCIAL WORK

Introduction

> One should teach physics rather than *about* physics . . . physics is not so much the *topic* as it is the mode of thought, an apparatus for processing knowledge about the nature rather than a collection of facts that can be got out of a handbook. Physics is not something that one knows about but is, rather, something one knows how to. . . . It is an approach to learning that emphasizes ways of getting from the surface of the observed to its underlying structure of regularity.
>
> Jerome Bruner

Social Work Training and Education: The Place of Skill

Education for social work arose in agency in-service training programs from the need of the charity agencies for some systematic means of training workers to offer the services. The early teachers of social work practice were agency-based practitioners who formulated practice theory out of their firsthand experiences in meeting clients and dealing with human need. As these practitioners moved into the teaching posts in the emerging schools of social work, the predominant educational pattern became a theory in the classroom and application of theory in the field, i.e., in field work in a social agency.

This applied portion of the learning experience occurred under the watchful eyes of the agency supervisor or field instructor according to whether agency or school was the actual employer. In either case, the partnership between school and agency was a close one and was devoted to the novice's learning experience out of the work with real live client(s). Rooted as this was in the demands of practice, the supervised field practicum was a classic example of experiential learning, an approach to learning highly valued now.

The craft and art of social work were passed on through a kind of apprenticeship arrangement. There were dedicated master teachers and devoted learners. Skill development was a laborious, painstaking

1

process that extended beyond the two years of graduate training and persisted throughout one's agency career. Eventually the diligent practitioner might advance to become a supervisor.

The predominant intellectual imperative facing the young schools of social work was to conceptualize a *professional* practice, i.e., to substitute practice wisdom for individual moral judgments. In these same years the profession was engaged in professionalizing itself, in seeking the components of a "real profession" which Abraham Flexner had claimed were lacking in 1915—a scientific base, unique method, communicable technique, uniform accreditation structure, professional associations and journals.

The schools were involved not only with the task of articulating theory for casework practice, but with developing congenial, teachable connections with the value base, social and psychological theories, social policy, and historical foundations. In short, a coherent curriculum within the social work MSW programs was the priority. Beyond this, when the social work programs became lodged in universities, they had to adapt to the rest of the university, to become more "scientific" and respectable in the eyes of the other professors in academia.

Traditionally, universities were devoted to providing a liberal education rather than a utilitarian or pragmatic education. Emphasis was placed on the contemplative/skeptical rather than the practical/doing, on the intellectual rather than the emotional or behavioral; and these priorities became the major concern of most professors. Conceptualizing the processes involved in learning or teaching held low intellectual appeal or status. The elements and dynamics involved in any kind of skill development were ignored or relegated to extracurricular activities (athletics, socials, special interest groups), to the academies (music, dance, art), to adult education and continuing education programs, and to vocational/technical schools.

Such was the historical orientation of Western thought and education: the respectable education was a liberal one, one not tied to a vocation or particular occupational objective. The less utilitarian the education the better. Higher education moved away from the concrete, the practical, the concern with skill. It favored the abstract, the theoretical, the concern with information. By tradition, the universities tended to value the scholarly, abstract, conceptual, rational words-and-numbers thinking in contrast to the emotive, intuitive, relational, affective, attitudinal modes of knowing and learning. Least valued was skill learning and development—the motoric, kinesthetic, and perceptual modes of experiencing and knowing.

Eastern thought, on the other hand, was not caught up in such dichotomies. It consistently placed great value on the role of knowing through direct, personal experience, on knowledge obtained through revelation as opposed to "scientific" investigation, and upon skill development as a noble pursuit. This essential difference between Eastern and Western approaches to education is captured by Suzuki in his description of skill mastery in Japan and Far Eastern countries:

> The arts are not intended for utilitarian purposes only or for purely aesthetic enjoyments, but are meant to train the mind. . . . If one really wishes to be master of an art, technical knowledge of it is not enough. One has to transcend technique so that the art becomes an "artless art" growing out of the Unconscious. . . . Man is a thinking reed but his great works are done when he is not calculating and thinking. "Childlikeness" has to be restored with long years of training in the art of selfforgetfulness. When this is attained, man thinks yet he does not think.[1]

The professions developed their own routes to skills acquisition, ordinarily delegating this chore to some apprenticeship or internship loosely linked to the educational institution. Social work, caught up in the priorities and ambiance of the university, attempted to fit in with the valued emphases and reward systems of higher education and the established professions.

Moving away from *training* to *education,* most social work programs gradually adapted to the intellectual influence valued in their host settings. Training by definition focused on proficiency in actions and performance achieved through instruction, practice, discipline, and drill. The desired outcome would be more or less uniform performances judged by some experts to be "good." Educating, on the other hand, implied an imparting of general knowledge, the development of powers of reasoning and judgment, and a focus on broader understanding of situations or contingencies as well as skill. A mark of an educated professional would be differentiated, self-directed practice.

The social agency became the place where the evolving practice theory (mainly of the casework method) might be applied and where skill should be learned. The school/agency relationship was a close one considered to be a partnership (so long as the agency met the school's requirements); but the guiding, dominating "partner" was the school.[2]

A New Focus on Skill

Due to the biases against skill teaching as inappropriate for "higher" education, this content was a relatively recent innovation in MSW programs. Not until the early 1970s were there special classes devoted to teaching skills. Sometimes the skills classes were designed as laboratory or workshop offerings with partial or no academic credit. Or perhaps skills practice was included as part of the practice class or the field seminar.

By the mid-1970s the social work profession and its education became concerned with the particulars of skill components and how to teach them. Bloom studied fifty evaluative procedures used in social work education studies and found skill to be the element receiving most attention (more than knowledge, values, and professional self-integration) as well as the element having the greatest diversity in modes of data collection.[3]

What caused such a sudden turnaround in educational emphasis? Several factors must be cited:

- A disenchantment with the cumbersomeness of traditional supervisory teaching, with its one-to-one approach which rested on reporting to the supervisor verbally and in writing about the experience. In the crunch of bureaucratic life, this mode of tutoring grew too costly and time consuming.

- Psychology moved out of the testing business as its main focus and moved into clinical work thus becoming competitive with social work for agency positions.

- Psychologists and other mental health professionals discovered interpersonal skill training packages that could prepare groups of learners more quickly to counsel others.[4]

- Training grant monies appeared for various professions and for training paraprofessionals to work in social and health delivery systems.

- A knowledge explosion in theoretical orientations and methods required new instructional modes. This was especially evident in the rise of group approaches (workshops and brief institutes) as well as in an increased emphasis on time-limited teaching/learning formats.[5]

- Social work not only competed with other professions for grants and contracts, but tripled its own educational auspices. The newly articulated BSW programs were eager to have skill training classes.

- Audio and video taping, a new electronic technology, and one-way screens offered opportunities to study and correct microbehaviors that were at the heart of newly conceptualized theories of verbal and nonverbal communication.

- Emphasis on goal setting, behavioral objectives, measurement, evaluation, and behavioral theory and research lent importance to skill training approaches.

These and other factors forced the social work educators to rethink their approach to skill development and spend increased attention on this matter. The NASW's 1977 Professional Symposium planning committee issued a call for papers for the 20th Anniversary that announced "join in reviewing the past, analyzing the present, planning for the future of *social work skill*." It promised that over 100 social work colleagues would present papers on the subject.[6] And yet, in the publication of selected papers from this conference, the word "skill" was edited right out of its title, *Social Work in Practice*.[7]

By 1978 a survey of interpersonal skills training in eighty-five graduate schools of social work revealed that 78 percent had two to four hours of weekly skills training classes which were offered for an average of eight to fifteen weeks. In thirty-two schools this was a required course.[8] Social work had joined mainstream thinking in sponsoring skills training for masters and bachelors level students.

Corporations were also attuned to having assessment centers and skill development programs for employees at the worker, managerial, and executive levels. And in 1978 the United States Congress added the Basic Skills Improvement Program as part of the Education

Amendment. *Speaking* and *listening* joined the three R's as basic skills to be taught in public schools.

The information revolution had forced awareness of the need for developing ways to cope with massive loads of data in all walks of life. Focus on and instruction in skills was now "in." What was needed were organizing typologies and labeling systems so that the components could be identified, differentiated, understood, practiced, and learned. Several possibilities were available.

Approaches to Conceptualizing Skills

Social work has used various approaches to defining and specifying skills:

Viewing skill as a global essence, the conscious use of self, as craft and art that expresses all that a "good" social worker knows and does. In this orientation skill was defined as embodying four components: knowledge, action, intentions/values, and style.[9]

Using such terms as "skill in interviewing," "skill in observation" and so forth. These process terms more accurately label activities, tasks, roles, or functions, and beg the issue of specifying the particulars. They are part of the global essence orientation.

Describing general skills and specific techniques [10] or tactics [11] that go with a particular method. Here skill is equated with excellence in understanding the method and in using prescribed techniques within the method to express the goals and values of social work.

Developing conceptual frameworks that link skills with particular practice roles as a preliminary to specifying skill components.[12]

Constructing typologies. Two main orientations were followed: specifying basic worker movements [13] or identifying needed worker qualities.

These typologies of components may have been called interactional techniques, behaviors in skill areas, or constitutuent subroutines. In any case, the skill-area was broken down into small entities thought to combine into an action or a quality. These two traditions will be considered in greater detail. They are at the heart of most skill training approaches and are antecedent to the skills approach that will be presented in this book.

Human Relations Orientation: Interpersonal Skills or Helper Qualities

One main orientation, human relations, viewed certain qualities of the helper as critical for attaining skill in the interpersonal area. In 1947 the T (Training) Group began as the BST group or Basic Skills Training Group which focused on diagnostic and action skills for change agents, group members, and leaders. Skill practice via role playing was a major emphasis. But soon this skills emphasis was eliminated in favor of a focus on the here and now, on studying the group's processes, on social interaction, perceptual accuracy, and awareness of others' reactions to one's self. This emphasis grew to become known as sensitivity training and eventually as personal growth groups. In the 1960s a whole new self-awareness industry began to flourish.

In Great Britain Michael Argyle was an early explorer of the interpersonal skills arena, perhaps among the first to conceptualize the sequencing of individual interactional behavior as a kind of serial motor skill not unlike driving, piano playing, or typing.[14] His categories of social competence included perceptual sensitivity, warmth, and rapport. In his repertoire of "social techniques" were flexibility, energy and initiation, and smooth response patterns. Argyle was concerned with "professional social skills"—speaking, teaching, supervision, selling, survey interviewing, and so forth as well as social skills training.

In the United States Carl Rogers was influential, especially in clinical psychology. His conceptual orientation saw key components of helping as *product* (of the helper's behavior), as specifying how one should behave in order to have a constructive impact on the client—the object of the counseling experience. For example, the expected outcome might be concreteness or respect. Emphasis was on the qualities of the helper which would differentiate successful from unsuccessful help. These qualities were designated by *descriptive nouns,* e.g., sensitivity, openness. Rogers' "therapeutic triad" of empathic understanding, unconditional positive regard, and congruence,[15] and Truax and Carkhuff's training for accurate empathy, nonpossessive warmth, and genuineness,[16] which was derived from Rogers' work, are examples of the human relations orientation focused on helper qualities.

Manpower Orientation: Task Skills

A second major approach to formulating necessary skills derived from the manpower field and began with the components of the job. In this tradition emphasis was upon the *process* or function. The focus was upon the task and what must be done to accomplish it, rather than upon how it was accomplished. The vocabulary here uses *action verbs,* e.g. asks, listens, persuades, in order to provide specific behavioral descriptors of the actions needed to accomplish specific intended objectives.

Sidney Fine pioneered an approach known as Functional Job Analysis (FJA) in which jobs were classified with nested hierarchies of skill levels into three families according to function: dealing with people, data, and things.[17] Within each skill level, behavioral components were specified using illustrative tasks that defined aspects of the job expectations, arranged from low to high in terms of the degree of independent judgment required. For example, "asks client questions and listens to and records answers on standard housing information form" would be at the simplest level of the People Scale.

In addition to the *functional skill* families (people, data and things) that in combination classify various occupations, Fine also conceptualized *specific content skills,* i.e., those required for a particular job in an organization such as "using agency guidelines for interviewing clients," and *adaptive skills,* i.e., those behaviors related to self-management, use of time, appropriate dress, and so forth.[18] He wanted to avoid "global process terms" such as interviewing, counseling, and developing service plans, all of which contain a series of worker actions and interactions. Fine's work has been a great stimulus to others to specify concrete behavioral components.

The task analysis approach emphasizes components of working beyond mere interpersonal skills, although these are crucial. The skill components associated with a particular job's content and the behaviors connected with image management exert a profound impact on competence and connect with various social work roles. That is, while all social workers need interpersonal skills if their work depends upon dealing with others, the degree of importance of interpersonal skills varies with the particular role; e.g., such skills are more important to the clinician than to the policy developer.

Overview of Orientations to Skill

We have identified three major historical traditions in conceptualizing skill: as a molar entity derived from years of supervised experience, termed the purposeful (conscious) use of self; as a set of personality traits or qualities, or what the "good" practitioner needs to *be;* and as a molecular collection of entities extracted from analysis of the tasks to be accomplished, or what the "good" practitioner needs to *do.* A final, as yet underdeveloped approach, is a transactional view of skills. In such an approach entities would be derived from the context—the transaction(s) among worker, client(s), and the environment, or what the "good" practitioner needs to *construct* out of the emergent situation.

Obviously, different typologies of skill elements will follow from one's preferred definition of skill. Most emphasis in specific skills training classes since the 1970s has been devoted to the interpersonal skills realm following either a helper quality or task component orientation. A proliferation of training programs was accompanied by the spread of training from social work, psychology, and psychiatry to early childhood education, corrections, nursing, nutrition, and other fields. Kiel reviewed the skills literature in social work from 1965 to 1979. According to her analysis, the programs were welcomed by students and educators as one tangible means of developing confidence and competence.[19] She cited a possible danger in producing technical practitioners, yet saw the importance of a needed focus on the *how* as much as the *why* of practice.

A comprehensive review of interpersonal helping skills approaches

was undertaken by Kurtz and Marshall in a twelve-year study of 141
skills training programs offered in the 1970s and early 1980s.[20] In this
survey of skills training in counseling, medicine, social work, and
nonprofessional programs, 38 distinct skill labels were identified.
However, nine main skills were used: empathy, questioning, genuineness, respect, attending, reflection of feelings, confrontation, concreteness, and immediacy. In most cases the training was aimed at
beginners and it pursued basic rather than more subtle skills. The
training programs derived mainly from Roger's orientation and focused on one-to-one helping. No one model was seen as more effective than the others.

A Conceptual Approach to "Skills for Direct Practice"

We shall not review here the various skills approaches developed by
others. These can be found by the interested reader elsewhere.[21] The
orientation we follow in this book stems from the task analysis tradition, with an added touch of a preference for a constructionist view.
In other words, we believe skill is neither a function of personality nor
a global essence that must take years to develop and is identifiable
only after the fact. We aim to identify behaviors that need to be
learned. We also see the clients as playing their part in conditioning
what the practitioner should do to accomplish the task and we see the
environment (or situation) as another active agent conditioning what
should happen. Therefore, we shall present descriptions of skill components and also describe various conditions that should elicit their
enactment. We see skills as molecular behaviors that can be taught,
learned, and evaluated.

Practice principles provide elements for social workers to consider
in the performance of their professional assignment, and these limit
the range of alternative actions available to them.[22] The development
of social work skill involves learning to produce specific behaviors
through which the knowledge and values incorporated in, and organized by, the principles that guide practice can be applied in the
performance of tasks.

The skill areas (e.g., skills for dealing with feelings, skills for initiating change) and their sub-component behaviors are generic activities. These will be identified, described, and illustrated in subsequent chapters. They are the particular *how's* of practitioner activity that can fit with any practice model or approach. In other words, they help illuminate the *how-to* but not the *why* of the work.

The *why* of the work will derive from two sources. The practice principles from the worker's theoretical orientation provide direction for the work. Justification and intentionality stem from the values of the social work profession. The skills are the technical part of the work. They do not stand alone, for they would be mindless and heartless. They enable practitioners to do well, but do not determine that they will do good!

There is increasing recognition in the professional literature that much of what has been presented as worker behavior is more accurately a group of goals to which some unspecified worker behavior should be directed. But, as Briar and Miller indicate:

> Injunctions to "give support to the client" or to "clarify the client's feelings" are of little use unless the theory specifies, in terms of behaviors to be performed by the practitioners, how support may be given or how feelings may be clarified. . . . "Support" and "clarification" describe effects, not the actions to be taken to produce them. Such prescriptions amount to telling the practitioner to "make the client feel better," or "improve the client's social functioning."[23]

It is not sufficient to specify outcomes toward which unspecified behaviors should be directed. The behaviors must be specified, and the conditions that occasion their use must be explained. In terms of Argyle's wonderfully basic description of social interaction as the production of a series of noises and gestures in response to a series of noises and gestures produced by another,[24] the particular noises and gestures that the social worker should produce in response to particular noises and gestures produced by others under specified conditions must be made explicit. The effort here is to specify behavior through which social workers in direct or face-to-face practice can apply the principles of their practice orientation in response to the demands of people needing help with various problems and to the broader social imperatives for a just society.

Skill Mastery Defined

As defined here, "skill" refers to the production of specific behaviors under the precise conditions designated for their use. In this sense, a worker cannot have more or less skill in producing a particular behavior. The worker either produces the behavior when the presenting conditions signal its use, or he does not. This approach to the concept skill differs from the more common usage having to do with proficiency in the performance of an act such as swimming, writing, or lecturing. However, acts such as swimming, writing, or lecturing to which the more common usage of the word "skill" is applied, are actually sets of smaller acts. Swimming includes arm and leg movements, head movements, breathing patterns, and so forth. It seems reasonable to assume that smaller acts, however, leave less room for degrees of mastery in performance. At some point there is a set of minute movements, each of which is either performed or not performed. As the number of movements involved in an act increases, on the other hand, some movements may be performed while other movements are not performed, resulting in some *degree* of mastery.

The worker can have more or less skill in a given skill area and the degree of skill that the worker demonstrates is measurable. Worker skill in a given area is a direct function of the number of specific behaviors in that area that the worker produces under appropriate conditions. A worker who produces six of the eight information-engagement behaviors when presenting conditions signal their use is 75 percent skillful in dealing with information. He is 50 percent more skillful than another worker who only produces four of the eight information-engagement behaviors under appropriate conditions.

It should be noted that production of a specific behavior under the precise conditions designated for its use involves two variables: knowledge and action. The worker must know the relationships between antecedent conditions, acts, and probable outcomes, on the one hand, and be able to produce the acts, on the other hand. It is one thing to know that, given conditions a, b, and c, the use of behavior x will probably result in outcome y. It is quite another thing actually to produce behavior x. While knowledge is necessary, it is not sufficient.

Both knowledge of the conditions under which x will probably result in y and the ability to produce x are required.

It follows that worker behavior can be viewed as hypothesis testing. In other words, every time the worker selects and produces a particular behavior, she is testing an hypothesis that the particular behavior she chooses will produce the effect she desires. It follows, too, that whenever the worker's hypothesis is not confirmed, she will need to consider whether failure to obtain the expected outcome was a function of chance, as untenable hypothesis, or her own inaccurate production of the behavior she had properly chosen.

Ryle highlighted the essence of possessing a skill: its intentionality.[25] He claimed a clown's cleverness may be shown in his tripping and tumbling. He trips and tumbles just as clumsy people, except that he does so *on purpose,* after much rehearsal and at the golden moment and where the children can see him. Skill at seeming clumsy are the works of his mind, are his jokes. A clumsy person does not trip on purpose. Tripping on purpose is both a bodily and a mental process. The skill is not what happens in the head or with the tongue, but what in action shows whether or not one knows the rules in the executive way of being able to apply them.

For us, the skills for social work practice are of the body, mind, and heart; and are piloted by the technical particulars, the practice principles, and the value base of the profession. And always, the resulting intentionality of the practitioner, whose aim is to work competently, is to produce the appropriate skill-component at the exact moment when the contextual situation (determined by others and the environment) signal NOW.

Skills for Direct Practice

In earlier times the social work profession dichotomized practice. There was direct and there was indirect practice. The *direct practice* meant front-line practice with the client or group where, according to *The Social Work Dictionary,* goals are reached through personal contact and immediate influence with those seeking social services. This was contrasted with *indirect practice,* activities aimed at achieving social goals or developing human opportunities.[26]

This distinction seems meaningless to us in the complexity of the present day service world, at least so far as these technical skills are concerned. The very *social* grounding of the social work profession requires *all* social workers must work toward immediate, particular goals, broader social goals, and especially, they must work for the extension of human opportunity. All practitioners assume various roles—conferee, broker, mediator, advocate—in pursuit of their professional assignment, which may involve diverse functions, e.g. assessing, planning, treating, supervising, administering, promoting, and so forth. All must deal with others as they pursue their ideas and plans at whatever level.

Perhaps a continuum best characterizes the work: a more or less mixture of skills for dealing with persons, information, and things. For our purposes here we see the direct practice skills described in this collection as basic to the work of *all* practitioners.

We have imposed an arbitrary order on the vast array of behavioral components in skill areas that made sense to us. Hopefully, this arrangement will enable the reader to enter the complex area of skill with certain guide posts that simplify matters. We shall identify, define, and illustrate some of the skills; others may only need identification. Hereafter, we shall refer to the clusters of behavioral components as *skill areas* or Skills for Dealing with _____. And we shall identify each component behavior as a *skill.*

We make no claims that we have presented a complete typology. Different and other components are inevitable. This is a start and a direction.

Four categories of skills orient our thinking and form the basic organization of this book. *Inner skills* affect the internal decision making processes that affect the worker's mental preparedness to act. *Interactional skills* occur between the worker and other(s). *Group skills* are needed, in addition to those in the first two categories, when more than one other person is involved. *Strategic skills* are used in special situations.

Chapters 1 and 2 examine *perception skills* and *cognition skills.* These observational and assessment skills may or may not be obvious to an external observer, yet they are profoundly important since they condition and direct all that happens between the worker and other(s). These *inner skills* combine to make up one's frame of reference.

The *interactional skills* are those that are prominent in the transactions with others. These skills for dealing with transactions between the worker, other(s), and environmental forces are identified within three skill areas: *skills for setting the stage, skills for dealing with information,* and *skills for dealing with feelings.* They are presented in chapters 3, 4, and 5.

Skills for working with groups are described in five chapters, chapters 6 through 10. Chapter 6, "About Groups," discusses why group work demands skills in addition to those needed for work with individuals. The group skills are further approached in chapter 7, "Continuous Group Skills," which considers skills which should always operate when working with more than one other person; and chapter 8, "Skills for Building Groups," and chapter 9, "Skills for Facilitating the Work of the Group," which consider skills which are used contingent upon the circumstance. Chapter 10, "Skills for Non-Talking Groups," introduces the special instances that require activity or experiential approaches as communicative modalities.

In the final section, "Strategic Skills," we introduce skills that are called for in certain special circumstances. Chapter 11 is "Skills for Dealing with Barriers," and chapter 12, "Skills for Dealing with Conflict."

Let us begin!

PART ONE

Inner Skills

1. Perception Skills

The husband of a woman whom Picasso was painting appeared at the studio one day. Picasso showed him the almost finished portrait and asked, "What do you think?" Using all of the tact that he could muster, the husband said, "Well . . . it isn't really how she looks." "Oh? And how does she really look?" Picasso asked. The husband then took a photo out of his wallet, handed it to the artist, and said, *"This* is how she looks," whereupon the artist, examining the photo, replied, "Hmmm . . . small, isn't she!"

Here and in chapter 2 we deal with what we term "inner skills." We call these "inner" in contrast to the "interactional" and "working with groups" skills, since these are the mental maneuvers that inform the worker's decisions to do this or that with an individual or group. They precede and should determine all of the worker's other actions. They are critical and enormously consequential. As social workers contemplate the helping situation and what should be done, these inner skills create a professional orientation. Their use also helps counteract the blind spots in the ordinary frame of reference—those largely unconscious, ingrained biases and misperceptions that automatically could affect the work in an out-of-awareness way.

Inner skills are those that deal with receiving incoming information and making sense of it. They make the difference between professional, disciplined help and the helping approaches of volunteers, of paraprofessionals, of neighbors or well-meaning friends. They make the work *social work*.

The content areas in these two chapters are elusive ones; ordinarily they are omitted from typologies which aim to specify communication skills. More often the focus is on those interactional skills which can be seen and counted as they are used. These skills, on the other hand, are hidden. They form a mind-set.

It is hard to draw a line that separates perception from cognition. The two areas are intertwined and have been dealt with variably in literature, poetry, philosophy, psychology, aesthetics, science, and in religious and spiritual writings. Sometimes "I perceive" has been used to equate with "I know." At times "I see" can mean "I think." Even "I feel" gets confused with "I think" as when a person says, "I feel *that* we should go." Nevertheless, we shall attempt a dividing line that makes sense, at least pragmatically, in terms of what social workers might see, think, and do. We "see" this attempt at identifying and describing inner skills as a beginning move in an uncharted area which may lead others to identify other skills in the future.

Perception Awareness

Consider the old adage: "Seeing is believing." This should be turned around to become "Believing is seeing!"[1] For, what we believe will condition what we allow ourselves to look at and therefore what we see. Our belief system is formed by at least three influences: our information processing style, which affects how we deal with information (e.g. analytic vs. global, convergent vs. divergent);[2] our culture-based values, ethics, and overall world view (e.g., present vs. future oriented, optimistic vs. pessimistic, achievement vs. relationship oriented);[3] and our profession or discipline-based conventions about "right" and "wrong" ways to "know" (e.g., using empirical, pragmatic, or experiential approaches). These combine to form our *perspective* or point of view which limits our seeing: we see what we expect to see.[4]

Everyone has developed a belief system, a perspective which operates to guide one's course through the vicissitudes of living. Having a point of view about self, others, and the environment provides a general orientation of prearranged ideas that keeps one's world in order. This system of ideas, feelings, and predispositions brings comfort and order, linkage to one's own and others' culture and environment, and continuity of tradition and learned notions about "reality." Perspective determines what has meaning and value, how much openness and difference one can tolerate, and what must be ignored or transformed because it doesn't fit with one's expectations or belief system. Mostly, our beliefs go unquestioned until we encounter others who are "different." It is then obvious that there are many ways of looking at things, not simply our way.

At a national level, for example, there looms the diversity between the world views of those in the United States and in Iran. At a more "back home" level, it is often the shared belief systems that lead to friendship and socializing choices as we "seek out our own kind." But professional practice allows for no such preferences. The social worker must learn to be open, to be sensitive to ethnic, racial, and cultural difference, must confront one's ordinarily unconscious belief system and bring its elements into conscious awareness. This is why perception-awareness becomes so important. We think of this as "disciplined looking," a set of behaviors that can be learned.[5]

What Is Perception?

In distinguishing perception from cognition it is helpful to consider the difference between *looking* and *seeing*. Looking is essentially a visual-perceptual experience. Seeing is a cognitive-embellished *outcome* of looking. We can look at something and not really *see* it! In fact we must not deal with all that we look at; we must screen out certain details lest we have stimulus overload. Babies learn early to develop a screening mechanism as a defense against stimulus overload, to sort out the important from extraneous sounds and sights.

What we (decide to) *see* depends upon our mental readiness, our previous experiences or viewings of comparable or contrasting images stored in memory that lead us to notice certain particulars of the "seen" (the scene) and to accord importance to these particulars.[6] It is the same for hearing. Listening is comparable to looking; hearing is comparable to seeing. To really hear is quite different from mere listening. One can listen but not hear. *Hearing* is the outcome of listening, just as *seeing* is the outcome of looking. To *hear* demands active attention devoted to dealing with the words that the brain receives, sorting through and selecting the key, meaningful words or themes.

Seeing and hearing are components of observation. It is striking how little attention is given to teaching observation as a practice skill. "Have we not been observing all our lives?" it could be argued. What is taught is presented ordinarily expositionally, i.e. cognitively, and more often as a research rather than as a practice imperative. Research classes exhort the learner to get one's biases out of the picture, to guard against observer bias. They also inform the novice about the pitfalls of the halo effect (attributing other positives to a person or thing on the basis of one observed, valued attribute). As the budding researcher learns to observe carefully and think critically, the halo effect is seen as contamination of the process. Observer bias is equally a contamination in practice! The same precautions are necessary to ensure an authentic practice act.

Perception and Cognition

The brain works to encode, select, retain, and transform information in order to make sense of incoming stimuli. That portion of these complex processes which can be thought of as perception is one specific component. It is automatic, fixed, and free from interference by other systems of the brain. Short of shutting the eyes or plugging the ears there is no way that consciousness (the learned, "higher" mental processes of cognition) can affect the raw data of the senses or alter the workings of the perceptual systems. These will apply willy-nilly, no matter one's immediate concerns.

However, perception involves more than mere sensory experience. The classical belief in five sensory receptors is more accurately described as five basic perceptual systems that encompass ten or more sense mechanisms, e.g., vestibular, visual, auditory, kinesthetic, tactual, pressure, pain, thermal, smell, and taste senses. These perceptual systems actively extract and combine information in order to give meaning to sensations. For example, seeing is the combined result of using ears, body muscles, and skin as well as the eyes.[7]

The chief role of perception is to keep us aware of local space and time and other immediate experiences, e.g., language comprehension, tasting, smelling, touching. It is not to deal with what is far off or what is past or in the future. Perception is confined to the present, to the split-second slices of the NOW. The key processes of perception in social work (the looking and listening) are insensitive to the thinking brain, which, as, we have remarked, transforms looking into seeing and listening into hearing.

In fact, what we know can be independent of what we see! This is the stuff of optical illusions and magic shows. We have tried to teach this subtle, but all-important point through various perception exercises for many years.[8] For example, consider these two lines of equal length:

We "know" they are equal in length and yet we look at them as different! It is much the same when we have planted a red ace of spades in a deck of otherwise "normal" playing cards and show about five cards to others. They "know" there is no such thing as a red ace of spades. So usually the viewers call this card "ace of hearts," and try to ignore the spade shape. There is no room in memory to receive a red ace of spades. But they also later confess to having a vague discomfort in doing so. Something is not quite right.

Cognition is voluntary. It is under the control of "higher" central systems which can manipulate information globally, range across mental domains, compare/contrast, reason by analogy, and so forth. Cognition depends on learning and experience. How one interprets the following picture,[9] whether it is a martini (with an olive dropping into it) or part of a bikini depends upon a person's prior learnings and preferences. But we *must* see it as a something!

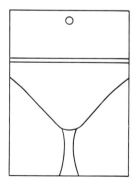

Unlike cognition which is fallible and idiosyncratic, perception is automatic and fixed. It is a sensory operation and is affected mainly by physiological capacities. That is, one notices more or less accurately according to the acuity of one's sense receptors.

If perception *is* automatic, then how can one learn perception skills? What can be taught and thus learned is to attend consciously, skeptically to matters of perception, *not* to trust one's senses so to speak! What can be learned is to question the validity of what one notices and to report without value-based embellishments the behavior that one observes. One can learn to work on remaining continually attentive to what is happening in the present moment, to avoid automatic habituation to sights and noises just because they are commonplace happenings. One can work against tuning-out! And what must be laboriously learned is to separate actual occurence from previous experiences or expectations.

We shall describe four skills which can contribute to disciplined looking: looking with planned emptiness, looking at the old as if new, jigsaw puzzling: leaving blanks for the story to unfold, and looking from diverse angles.

Looking with Planned Emptiness

To look with planned emptiness is deliberately to cultivate an area in one's mind that is reserved for the unknown, that is ready to accommodate the new, perhaps alien, idea and experience it, rather than rationalize it away or avoid it. By keeping and taking pride in the empty cell in the perception structure, it becomes impossible for one "not to see it" because one has no conceptual category for it (no red ace of spades). It is as prizing and valuing the holes in the swiss cheese, as recognizing that these very holes are a mark of the ripening of the total chunk that adds quality and subtlety to its essence.

In the past ideas lived longer than people. And once established, ideas would change only slowly and over several generations. Today technology and science have speeded up the rate of change so that people live longer than ideas and they must change their ideas within their lifetimes. A cultivated area of emptiness is one route toward being open to restructure or even discard ideas, rather than only building on the old ones.

Looking with planned emptiness implies recognizing the limits of one's knowledge, living comfortably with partial answers, and welcoming the doubting as well as the doing. It involves accepting uncertainty rather than dogma, allowing for intuitive and tacit knowings, and relishing inquiry. This means staying open, even in one's area of expertise, to the vast realms that may be unimaginable. "Why not?" becomes as important as "why?"

For social work practice, a key use of "planned emptiness" is not to let other workers' assessment of a client or situation precondition one's expectation of what will happen in *this* relationship! It is involved in the delicate maneuver of picking up someone else's case with a truly open mind.

Often, planned emptiness directs one to regard another's written assessments with skepticism and to adopt a "do-it-yourself" mentality so as to keep others' biases out "of your picture"! Consider this supposedly factual account describing Janet, a "short, stocky black woman who has been living at a state institution for the retarded for about twenty years":

> In a smaller group situation, she appears to be very happy, well-adjusted, and self-satisfied. However, with a closer analysis of Janet's behavior, her need for affection becomes apparent. She constantly hugs and kisses anyone who will let her. Her need to be wanted is obvious. She would rather help another person in the group than do her own work. She would rather scrub the sink or mop the floors than work on a project. If she feels that she has done something wrong, she cries to such an extent that it is hard to stop her. All of these needs point up Janet's one basic need for self-actualization.

Here is an instance where eager, novice workers must learn to ignore certain evaluations and conclusions. They must learn to regard the written record of service as fallible, as not etched in concrete! And mainly, they need to become able to separate descriptions of behavior from value-based evaluations of it. *In the above excerpt one must not believe that "Janet's one basic need (is) for self-actualization."*

In the following instance the social worker exhibits looking with planned emptiness.

While working on the Renal Dialysis Unit at University Hospital, I was making rounds with the physician when one patient in my case load called me back to her chair. She said she had read my memo to the ward concerning a new group forming "to recognize individual birthdays and have a fund for extending our expression of sympathy when a dialysis patient <u>dies</u>." Mrs. Kent said she wanted to know if I could have used another word in place of "dies" in that sentence. As she talked she kept apologizing for approaching me about the word. <u>I was caught off guard but I said nothing for a few moments and nodded as she talked. I wondered what the word "dies" might mean to her</u> and pulled a chair over to sit near her. <u>I sensed she wanted conversation at this time, because most of the time she pretends to be asleep. I sat there quietly.</u> She want on to say she didn't mind the word "die," but some of the other patients might find it hard to deal with.

In another instance, the social worker was on week-end duty in a de-tox program for substance abusers. Some of the residents talked her into sending out for pizzas. They promised this was allowed in the house rules.

I was new at this residence and had no reason to doubt what the residents said they could do on weekends. When they approached me with their boredom, <u>I thought for a moment and then said, "Why not!"</u> It was only several days later that I discovered the regular staff did not believe them when they said <u>I</u> (not they) had ordered the pizzas. <u>I had been open to their request and trusted them.</u> When I was reached after returning to the city, they were relieved when I clarified that I did, indeed, order the pizzas. <u>I did not think they were out to con me and they fulfilled my trust.</u>

Looking at the Old As If New

To look at the old as if new involves a playful attitude, one that can imagine and pretend. It is an optimistic stance. The seemingly impossible might just be possible. There are no "n'er-do-wells" nor total failures in one's case load, no matter how dismal their plight may seem to be at first glance.

In the words of Gordon, one needs to "sustain a childlike willingness to suspend adult disbelief. . . . To make the familiar strange is to distort, invert, or transpose the everyday ways of looking and responding which render the world a secure and familiar place. . . . It is the conscious attempt to achieve a new look at the same old world, people, ideas, feelings, and things." [10]

The social worker who looks at the old as if new strives to cultivate naivete, an "out of focus" look at some aspect of the known world, a willingness to tolerate ambiguity, and a readiness to take risks. This cultivated childlike honesty and openness involves telling the Emporer he is naked no matter the others' appreciation of his new clothes. It also involves looking with a "what if?" and "supposing? . . ." as much as with a "why."

The following instance shows a social worker willing to look at the old as if new:

> I wanted to start a support group for chronic mentally ill adults and proposed this idea at a staff meeting of the Outpatient Services Department. I was not prepared for the response that greeted this proposal. There were all kinds of reasons offered for not starting. For example: it was hard enough to keep up with our mandated services; mentally ill adults need more structure than that type of group; we are not reimbursed for such groups; and they wouldn't come just for vague "support." I was silent. I imagined there were some in our caseloads who were capable of increased independence and consistency if given the chance. I was surprised at the doom and gloom emphasis in the discussion. Was this burnout on the part of staff? I could see that my plan would not be supported by the others. I made a comment that seemed to surprise, "I'd like to give this a try and am willing to take this on in an after-hours assignment. I'd like to try with about eight persons and would appreciate any referrals made out of your case loads that you think might be able to be in such a group." Silence . . . and nods of assent.

Jigsaw Puzzling

Jigsaw puzzling entails leaving blanks for the story to unfold. The social worker who has cultivated "looking with planned emptiness" will also fairly easily adopt a stance that leaves room for the clients to fill out their "tales" at their own pace. The behavior involved here is trusting the client to reveal the important matters in her own way, taking the time needed to put the client at ease (despite time pressures), and adopting an inviting, non-threatening, stance.

The exchange between client and social worker should not feel like an inquisition or one-way interrogation. Nor should the worker collect "facts" irrelevant to the purpose of their meeting, no matter one's curiosity nor the client's eagerness to spin out the particulars.

A major evidence of this orientation is silence on the part of the worker, a deliberate silence plus attention to all that the other wishes to say (or not say). It is the cultivation of an unhurried, inviting, respectful atmosphere, an ambiance that accents the other's control over what will be shared in the situation. In the following instance, the supervisor used jigsaw puzzling in her approach to Jenny, one of her supervisees:

> I was impressed with Jenny's work. Since she joined our team six months ago, she has always had her reports in on time. She was on top of her case load, and, if anything, was almost too perfectionistic. I wondered why she never had lunch with any of us though, and why at our Christmas party she abruptly ran off as soon as she ate. I said nothing about it though, as it was none of my business for one thing, and for another, I figured that she would talk about this if and when she wanted to.
>
> A month ago at our evaluation conference Jenny asked me if I could recommend a therapist to her—she confided that she suffered from bulimia.

The next illustration also shows jigsaw puzzling on the part of the social worker.

> Rhonda was a recovering alcoholic. I saw her for six months, mainly dealing with her depression and lack of self-esteem. It was a break-

through when she told me she had been raped by her cousin when she was eleven. This had been a family secret she never discussed. But several months after this revelation, she still was pretty much on the same plateau as before. I wondered about what still seemed an air of secrecy about her, but did not question her on this, figuring she needed more time to face certain memories. Then one day she surprised me when she said at the start of the session, "I had a terrible flashback yesterday. She paused. After some heavy silence, she said, "my grandfather touched and fondled me when I was about two."

In another instance, the social worker is meeting with James, a thirty-two-year-old man with AIDS who has just moved into Walnut House:

James was angry but relieved. He said he was scared of being here, of living with others who had AIDS since he was ordinarily a loner, and frightened of what was ahead for him. But he said, "I know I'm lucky too; not everyone can get into a place like this. And I have no one I can count on." I was curious about how he got AIDS since he seemed so isolated. But I sat on my curiosity since this was not necessarily information for me to have.

Looking from Diverse Angles

To look from diverse angles is another way to keep open to the new and unexpected as well as to avoid snap judgments and the consequences of mistaken first impressions. It is a hang-loose mental attitude that appreciates the caution of Gilbert and Sullivan: "Things are seldom what they seem. Skim milk masquerades as cream."

The social worker looks from diverse angles figuratively and literally so as to avoid premature judgments and self-fulfilling prophecies. As much as possible, she sits on her expectancies and withholds evaluation to minimize the chance of stereotyping people or situations.

A diverse angle perspective is a precaution that counters "believing is seeing." We see what we expect to see unless we deliberately guard against these expectations. This can be accomplished by conscious attention to our tendency to categorize and label. One must learn to live with ambiguity rather than certainty and to tolerate contradictions. Social work is a profession with features of "uncertainty, instability, uniqueness, and value conflict"—situations which Schön described as needing reflective practitioners.[11]

The social worker tries to view situations from various perspectives, realizing that no two persons see exactly the same thing. She seeks others' viewpoints, yet buys into no special "side" before entertaining a wide spectrum of possible visions. Such a stance is especially crucial in work with families, in conflict situations and mediation efforts, and in group or committee work where all the individuals want their viewpoint to matter. It is a stance toward discovery of information which Bateson goes to great lengths to describe as "double or multiple comparison," a kind of binocular vision,[12] and Bruner sees as looking "as with the stereoscope," a circumstance in which "depth is better achieved by looking from two points at once."[13] It is a stance which also leads one to seek a second opinion when serious medical interventions are suggested.

The following excerpt brings looking from diverse angles to life:

> Mrs. Corey was at her wits end in trying to get Danny to mind her and get along with his younger brother, Bob. She complained of the constant fighting, with Danny being a bully. "Although Dan is seven and only one year older than Bob, I am afraid he will seriously injure Bob," she said. "Danny gets so angry whenever they are together." Mrs. Corey then said she was considering declaring Danny unmanageable. She wanted my support for this decision. I asked her if Danny gets into fights at school like he does at home. She said she didn't know, so I suggested we talk with his teachers and with Danny himself before taking any such action. Mrs. Corey seemed irritated by my caution. I said I knew it could be annoying to put off doing something about a troublesome situation, but that Danny might not act at school the way he does at home, and if that's the case, there may be other ways to prevent him from fighting with Bob at home.

Home visits are also important for getting a different angle on a client's situation. For some clients, coming to meet in "the office" automatically puts them on the defensive. It is a foreign territory. They will act differently at home. Other perspectives may be obtained through accompanying a client on a walk in the park, seeing the client in the family context, or participating in some special activity, e.g., a party, a trip. Often it is just such an "excursion" that will bring to light certain strengths, interests, feelings of esteem, or a vital but previously avoided issue.

Perhaps the most sweeping import of looking from diverse angles is the adoption of a mentality that sees the donut as well as the hole, the drinking glass both as half filled and half empty. For social workers, this means seeing client strengths as well as problems, seeing potential as well as consequences, and helping clients to do the same.

To continue with a photographic metaphor which "looking from diverse angles" suggests, two special maneuvers are components of such a view: *zooming* and *using a wide-angle lens*. In other words, at times the social worker steps forward to get a closer look or a magnified view. At other times she steps back to find the bigger picture, i.e., to do justice to the context in which the particular is embedded. These two special views distinguish an orientation with individual clients from one that must be assumed in working with groups in order to be sensitive to the groupness of the group. Each instance requires the worker to "see" differently, formulate different perceptions from sensory experience, and conceptualize differentially what is seen.

When working with an individual, one searches for the person. The picture of the client at any given moment is usually taken with a zoom lens. Just as one squints to gain a clearer view of a point of interest, so does the social worker zoom to sharpen her focus and capture the small detail. She highlighted the subject, placing it in the accented foreground and relegates the extraneous detail to the background.

On the other hand, when working with a group, one mainly searches for pattern. The social worker's attention is directed to the patterns of interaction among the persons, the properties of these patterns, and the locus and impact of each person within and in relation to these patterns. The picture of the group at any given moment must be taken with a wide-angle lens. This holds true for work with families and, in fact, for all work with more than one person at a time. When the context shifts to involve several persons at once, the worker's vision must shift also to encompass these transactions. Further discussion of what the worker must do in following a group-based perspective and using a wide-angle lens is elaborated in part 3, "Skills for Working With Groups."

In the following excerpt, the social worker zooms and in doing so corrects her first impression:

> When I met with Mr. Gold, I was brought up to date on the events of the past week. He was told by his supervisor that his department was being closed down; he would have two terminal weeks. Not only this, Mrs. Gold announced that she was leaving him. She said she always knew he was a loser. To top it all off his mother suffered a severe heart attack that same week and he was the only person she could count on to take care of the emergency. I said, "Gee, Mr. Gold, these are terrible things!" I waited. "Yes," he said. "I have a hell of a lot to do now." I mentally thought he was in crisis and probably would need to see me several times in the next two weeks. I figured I would have to help him mobilize his energies to deal with all these set-backs. I said, "You have a lot of set-backs happening now." Mr. Gold agreed and then began enumerating the things he had gone about doing: reviewing the want ads and getting his resumé in order; visiting his mother and helping her prepare for her discharge from the hospital; shopping and cooking his meals, trying to get to some different agreements with his wife who had moved in with her sister. He reported all this with an unruffled sense of confidence and busyness. I listened to his plans and actions and modified my first sense of alarm. What had seemed to be a crisis probably wasn't felt as a crisis to him. He was coping quite well.

Another example of zooming is this instance of the social worker meeting with Miss Carpenter who suffered from cancer of the liver:

> Miss Carpenter was emaciated. Her abdomen was quite distended. She was bent over and walked laboriously. She was depressed. She said she was a working person all her life, had worked at the General Electric plant for twenty-four years. She missed her friends at work. I wondered to myself why this should now be her preoccupation. She seemed so sad. From her physical appearance I assumed she must have left her job three or four months ago and would have adjusted by this time to being at home. I said, "It is hard to be cut

off from good friends." Then I added, almost as an aside, "How long since you left G.E.?" Two weeks. <u>I then realized that her new loss and grief was to be expected and modified my approach to help her deal with the losses.</u>

The zoom view or close-up vision can shed light on otherwise obscure feelings, behavior, and situations. Such careful attention to the ambiguities will yield more accurate assessments and quality moves by workers.

The wide-angle lens is also a must at times if one seeks to be in tune with the clients. In the following instance the social worker, an outreach worker from a Settlement House, meets with a streetwise group of twelve- and thirteen-year-old boys who are not interested in being part of the agency's in-house program.

> After three months of doing various sports activities, the attendance began to be fairly consistent. There were releatively few conflicts. I thought basic reliability and trust were being established in a safe context. And their behavior, while troublesome to the community, was not volatile within the group. This week was different. They tried all kinds of ways to frustrate me: they wouldn't get out of the car, they pretended they had lost the dues money, and they honked the car horn maliciously. Whatever rules we had made in the past were ignored.

> <u>At first I thought that I had perhaps done something to make them angry. I was tempted to ask them what I had done to make for all this "static" today. But then I thought about the expected stages of group development that groups are supposed to go through. I realized this was part of a "power and control" stage and told myself we would just have to go through this until we might get to an "intimacy" stage later on.</u>[14] <u>Looking at it this way made me realize the fighting and teasing were not a personal thing against me.</u>

Looking with a wide-angle lens is a necessity in team meetings, whether one is in the position of chairperson or team member.

> <u>I noticed in our team meetings that Sam usually said nothing unless directly questioned and Jerry always waited for Dick to give an opinion or suggestion. Then Jerry would voice an opposite opinion.</u>

I figured we wasted a lot of time going through a routine like this. It usually played itself out O.K. but we would spend about ten minutes looking at Dick's and Jerry's positions, finally wearing down and deciding to go this or that way. It was aggravating. I got up my courage and voiced this pattern that I had noticed. It was like an electric shock. Jane, today's chairperson, seemed pleased. The team talked a few minutes about how they might give everyone a chance too express opinions and still become more efficient.

These four skills — looking with planned emptiness, looking at the old as if new, jigsaw puzzling, and looking from diverse angles have been explored to offer ways to "see" more accurately in working with others. These perception skills condition judgments of meaning, the cognitions that will direct the work. We turn to cognitive skills in the next chapter.

2. Cognitive Skills

> The lines of play [in chess] that we foresee and try in our heads
> and dismiss are as much a part of the game as the moves that we
> make.
>
> Jacob Bronowski

Preceding, accompanying, and underlying every intervention in social
work are complex thought processes, cognitive activity directed toward
understanding clients and situations, choosing appropriate interventions, and preparing one's self to act. Since cognition is not directly
observable, it is difficult to isolate the many specific skills the social
worker must use. But it is possible to describe some of them. Six that
seem essential are recognizing feelings, looking for patterns of behavior, drawing inferences, hypothesizing, connecting the new to the
known, and reflecting on the work. These six cognitive skills are
discussed here and illustrated where possible with case material in
which social workers recorded their thoughts as well as their actions.

Recognizing Feelings

To recognize feelings, the social worker must attend to and notice the
many subtle and not so subtle ways that people manifest emotion
without words. Further, the worker must have a large and varied
vocabulary of feeling terms so that she can conceive of a broad range
of feelings and distinguish one from the other where nuance is critical. Within the general category of emotion characterized by fear, for
example, a person may feel jittery, hesitant, frightened, alarmed, pan-
icky, even terrified. An angry person may be perturbed, annoyed, or
furious. These are not synonymns, but qualitatively different emotional experiences. And the social worker who is attuned to these
differences is capable of the differential empathy that gives clients

that special sense of having been truly understood, for that worker can pinpoint the precise term that characterizes the client's inner experience.[1]

In the following example, the social worker recognizes two different types of fear that the client is probably experiencing.

> Rita is a seventeen-year-old mother whose month-old baby was hospitalized. The cause of the illness is unknown. Her first baby had drowned, and she was a suspect. She sat in silence in the hospital waiting room, shaking her leg up and down. Before I walked over to talk with her, I thought about what she might be feeling. I figured she was probably nervous about the baby and terrified of getting locked up again.

Once the social worker recognizes the particular emotions the client is probably feeling, she is able to express real empathy. Skills for expressing empathy are discussed and illustrated in chapter 4. Here, the focus is on cognition, so attention is given to the clues which feelings can provide, clues to the nature of salient problems the client may be facing, clues that can serve as a point of departure to guide systematic inquiry into the client's broader plight.

Sadness, for example, is generally associated with felt loss. The thing that was lost may be a significant object or person, a valued intangible such as someone's love or trust, or a quality of self, such as pride. The loss could be of a particular status, such as a managerial role in the workplace. The loss could even be of something one never actually had, such as a promotion given to someone else, but which one had expected to receive one's self. The social worker who recognizes that a person is feeling sad and knows that sadness is generally evoked by felt loss can not only empathize with the client, but can, after communicating her empathy, immediately probe for the loss.

Frustration is usually felt when obstacles are encountered on the way to a desired goal. In the example below, the social worker recognizes the frustration of a fourteen-year-old accident victim, expresses empathy, then asks about the goal and the obstacle.

> Sara said she wanted to see me, so I went over to the rehab. unit where she was getting physical therapy for her legs. When I saw her, she told me that every time this week she tried to show her

mother that she could walk with just a cane, she fell down, and now her mother doesn't believe her. She had a kind of defeated look and seemed weary. I figured that she was frustrated, so I said, 'That can be frustrating!' She said it was, and I nodded. Then I asked her what it was she wanted that she can't have if her mother doesn't believe she can walk with just a cane. She said she wants to live at home, but can't as long as she needs her mother's help getting around.

Looking for Patterns of Behavior

A behavior pattern is a series of movements that recur under a particular set of circumstances with little variation over time. To look for patterns of behavior, the social worker sorts through the many stimuli that comprise an interaction to see if its central elements match the central elements of other interactions.[2] If they do, then the current situation is a type of situation, and the social worker knows to use in this situation the intervention generally used in situations of this type.

In the example below, a social worker in child protective services picks up a pattern in the behavior of one of her clients.

> On Friday, Ms. Ridly called me and in a very upset voice said she didn't have enough money for milk for the baby's formula over the weekend. Last Friday she was very upset and needed money to pay something toward the electric bill so they'd have heat over the weekend, and the Friday before that she was upset over not having bus fare for James to go the library on Saturday to get his homework done.

In the following example, a social worker at a home for delinquent boys identifies a pattern of behavior that enables her to intervene quickly and appropriately. Had she not seen the boy's behavior as typical of a pattern, her intervention would have taken a very different direction.

> Brian was scheduled to be released next week after completing the behavior management program in only four months, so I was a little surprised to be told, when I got to work this morning, that he had

punched out another boy. He had been determined to get released in the shortest possible time in order to graduate with his class at the high school in his neighborhood, so I figured he'd be pretty disappointed about having another month tacked onto his stay.

I was on my way over to his dormitory to help him deal with his disappointment when I remembered that it isn't unusual for people in custodial facilities to act up just prior to their scheduled release time out of fear that they won't cope well or won't be accepted on the outside. So I shifted my focus and decided to reach for any fear about getting out that he might be feeling. When I did that, his eyes filled up. He thought they'd look at him funny at school.

Drawing Inferences

Sometimes people protect themselves from being vulnerable by not saying all that they mean or wish to say. Sometimes people are unsure themselves of what they really mean. And sometimes people do not catch the implications of their experiences because they are so busy experiencing them. Whatever the reason, people often leave out pieces of information crucial to their getting real and lasting help. When this happens, the social worker must try to fill in the missing pieces, which is to say, the social worker has to draw inferences.[3]

It should be noted here that an inference is a statement that has not yet been confirmed or disconfirmed. Thus, by definition, the social worker does not know if the inference she has drawn in any given instance is accurate or inaccurate. So it is incumbant upon her to check each inference for accuracy. Checking out inferences is discussed in chapter 5. Here we consider drawing inferences, the cognitive aspect of the process.

In the example below, a social worker at a mental health center draws an inference which, when checked out with the client, precipitates a dramatic shift in the direction of the work.

I started seeing Cathy Randell two weeks ago when she presented herself as depressed. It looked as if her depression was precipitated by fears of being alone during her roommate's impending six-month study tour. But today I learned that except for the last three months that she has been living with Andrea, she had been living alone for six years. When I pointed this out to her, she began to cry and said that was what scared her so much, that she must be falling apart. I <u>had a hunch something else was happening because of her fear of being alone when she's used to being alone and because she talked about Andrea with the kind of tenderness I sometimes feel toward my wife.</u> So I checked out my inference by saying, "Cathy, you're in love with Andrea, right?" "Oh my God," she said. "Oh my God."

Hypothesizing

In social work, every practice act is based on a hunch or hypothesis that by doing that act, some change for the better will result. In the example above, the social worker apparently hypothesized that by drawing and checking out his inference, the client would know more than she did before. In the example below, the social worker hypothesizes that summarizing, a skill elaborated in chapter 5, will bring a group that has strayed from the topic back to the work that needs to be done.

The Parents Advisory Board had been deliberating about whether or not to allow seventh graders to attend the Monday night dances held in the school gym when Mr. Stone started talking about the cable TV movies that are on when the children come home from school. He said he was hoping some of the other parents would join him in meeting with the local cable company to get them to change their 3 p.m. to 8 p.m. program lineup. Mrs. Wagner said she and her husband tried that last year and were told the cable company had nothing to do with the programming. Soon many other parents got in on discussing TV problems. <u>I thought that maybe if I summarized what we had talked about so far regarding whether or not seventh grades should come to the dances, the group might get back on track.</u>

Connecting the New to the Known

Connecting the new to the known is an understanding process. The social worker tries to understand what is happening in the moment by comparing and contrasting what she sees and/or hears with situations already familiar to her.

With experience in various situations over time, workers gradually build a fund of information, sometimes referred to as practice wisdom, to draw upon in meeting each new situation. And while each client and each situation is to some extent unique, there still are kernels of connections between the former experiences and the new confronting situation.

To connect the new to the known is to find the familiar in each new encounter and, at the same time, leave room for aspects never before encountered. Schön referred to this type of behavior as "reflection-in-action," by which he meant using one's repertoire of examples, images, understandings, and actions—the whole of one's experience to the extent that it is accessible—for understanding and action.[4] It is to see *this* as *that*, to make sense of a unique situation by seeing it as something already present in one's mental repertoire.

As a process, connecting the new to the known is somewhat similar to looking for behavior patterns. But it differs from the latter in two distinct ways: the nature of the content and the focal unit. In connecting the new to the known, the worker's focus is on more transitory phenomena. The content of concern is moment-by-moment action and interaction rather than recurrent action motifs. It further differs from looking for behavior patterns in that the search does not focus on the client. It focuses on the worker's prior interaction with other clients and non-clients which may shed light on what this client is experiencing right now.

In the example below, the social worker's experience with other people leads her to connect a slightly breaking voice on the telephone with a need for her to make a home visit then and there, despite the client's indication that she had other things to do and the visit could wait. Note that the worker labels her own behavior "pushy." We call it good social work.

I called Mrs. Holmes from a pay phone about a block from her house to see if a visit would be convenient for her. It was about ten days after her husband's death. She hesitated a second, enough for me to think that maybe it wasn't convenient for her after all. I asked her about my impression, and she acknowledged that she was about to leave to take some insurance papers to her doctor's office for him to sign. I told her that I could come another time, that I had just wanted to see how she was getting along. At that, she said, "I'm not sure . . . ", and her voice broke just slightly. So I did something that I don't do very often — get a little more pushy about coming on over right then. I said, "Why don't you let me come on over just for a little while . . . ? Maybe I can help some with the insurance things — and I won't stay long if you need to go on." She agreed, so I hurried to the house.

We sat down at the kitchen table where she had been working, and I asked how she was coming along; she told me about some of her confusion, and I answered a question or two for her. Then as she asked me another question, she started to get tears in her eyes, and I suggested we go sit on the sofa for a while. As she got up from the table, she began to cry more, and said, "I feel so weak," and tried to stop crying. I said, "You just sound human to me," and touched her arm. We sat down on the sofa and talked for a while about her feelings of loneliness and of being overwhelmed with new responsibilities for things she didn't understand. I talked some about the kinds of feelings many people have after losing a spouse, and about how she probably didn't have much energy just then for learning complicated new tasks. I helped her get finished with things that couldn't wait, and wrote down how for her to sort out things that needed immediate attention from things that could wait a few weeks, and made a date to come back then and help her go through those things. Then we talked some more about her husband and about her missing him. It turned out that she didn't need to make the trip to the doctor's office after all, and she was glad to have had the chance to talk about the things that were uppermost in her mind—the pain of her loss. I left after about an hour, and was glad I had been pushy.

Reflecting on the Work

Perhaps the ultimate cognitive skill is self-reflection. That is, as part
of each encounter, the social worker assesses what happened and
what did not happen, what might have happened or what should have
happened in the search for quality practice.[5] To reflect on the work is
to review one's intentions—the thoughts, feelings, and actions—and
to compare these to the outcomes of the engagement as one means of
confirming or correcting the effort. It is through such continuous self-
assessment that the worker knows and tests her quality in each parti-
cle of the work.

Our "internal gyroscope" strives to keep us on course. It is ani-
mated by our pride and desire for accomplishment through the work.
Mainly, we self-correct or confirm out of the process of negative
feedback. For example, if a teacher notes that the listeners are nodding, he raises his voice, speeds up his lecture, or in some other way
alters his delivery. And when a social worker notes that the course of
the work is static or repetitive, she reflects on the work and makes
adjustments in what she and thus they are doing together.

Unexamined work all too easily may become doctrinaire or routine.
In time, unexamined work also becomes boring. Its sameness and
mass-production mentality quickly loses the novelty and the mystery
that should characterize all work with people. For it is the blessing
and the burden of being human, in contrast to being alive (as are
plants and other animals), that we can be self-aware. We think about
our thinking, our feelings, and our actions. We are aware of our
frailties and our finitude. This is our existential condition—one that
leads us to seek meaning, to be reflective rather than mechanical, and
to want to make a difference using the opportunities we have.

Social work practice is alive with indeterminacies, complexities,
and value conflicts. To make sense of these uncertainties of practice
and do what needs to be done requires vigilance, imagination, optimism, and daring, as well as all the specialized knowledge that one
has accumulated. In short, it is through reflecting on the work that
the social worker aims to deal competently with the practice tasks.

PART TWO

Interactional Skills

3. Skills for Setting the Stage

There's language in her eyes,
   her cheek, her lip,
Nay, her foot speaks; her
   wanton spirits look out
At every point and motive of
   her body.

                        William Shakespeare

Stage setting is the beginning. Included here is social worker behavior aimed at launching the interaction process. At the outset of every human exchange the worker's objectives include making the physical environment (spatial arrangements, privateness, setting) conducive to the anticipated interaction; and providing a social-emotional environment congenial to connection or rapport. A theatrical metaphor has been used by others concerned with social interaction—"actors" in real-life "dramas,"[1] and stage setting. Such language appropriately directs attention to the set, the arrangements between worker and other(s) as the curtain rises.

Impressions begin on both sides as soon as the two parties are within visual range, and are continuously interpreted by each of the actors as signals of inviting or repelling intent. Through particular actions the worker can make a difference in the quality of each of the exchanges, whether with clients or with others in the service delivery system. In interactions with clients, the focus is upon the means through which the worker can increase client comfort. With respect to exchanges on a staff or interorganizational level, the focus may be upon the means through which comfort *or discomfort* of the other can be increased. Or the focus may be on ways to assume the initiative or control of the interaction. In general, the social worker enacts certain behaviors in order to set the stage in a particular way. These behaviors convey messages about how potentially responsive or unresponsive the worker may be, how pleasant or unpleasant the exchange may be, the size of the social barrier between worker and the other, and the role the worker may wish the other to assume.

Skills for setting the stage include the following three behaviors: positioning, engaging in the medium of the other, and proposing a medium presumably congenial to the other. We shall describe and illustrate these skills and then consider *attending,* a critical behavior that will continuously be used throughout all contacts with others, from the initial start of the exchange until the meeting ends and the other(s) is out of sight.

Positioning

To position is to place one's self physically at the distance and/or angle suitable for a particular type of interaction and to adjust one's self in accord with ensuing cues from the other as the interaction continues. Distance ranges for various levels of personal involvement have been found to follow culturally determined norms that differ within various cultures.[2] These norms, if violated, may be offensive to the other person. The appropriate space and other protocol behaviors must be known, respected, and observed if the worker is to make the other person feel comfortable. Studies of personal space, that private area surrounding the person which others may not enter,[3] indicate that intrusion affects feelings of comfort and status.[4] There is also evidence to suggest that what is felt as intrusion differs as a function of other variables. That is, if one person sits near another, it makes a difference whether there are other seats that could have been chosen, whether one is directly facing the other or at a right angle and whether there is any physical barrier between them.[5] Likewise, studies of groups reveal the importance of position at a table (as well as the shape of the table) with respect to leadership and dominance, the amount of communication that will be directed to an individual, and involvement with particular others.[6] Additional aspects involved in positioning pertain to the person of the worker: her facial expression, her body posture, the direction in which she looks, and her general orientation to the other.

In the following episode the worker deliberately arranges herself in a knee-to-knee informal position, one found to be preferred by interviewees.[7] She does not assume a more formal, face-to-face position, an arrangement found preferable for competitive situations;[8] and she avoids the desk, a potentially separating middle-class and business-like accouterment, out of her concern for client comfort and awareness that desks may be physical and cultural barriers to interaction.

> Mrs. Kyle came into my office and sat down. I moved my chair from behind the desk to cut down the psychological distance between us and sat near her.

In the next example, the worker initiates contact with a student in a classroom by assuming a side-by-side position, one used for very informal, transitory communications[9] as when watching and/or discussing something outside the individual. Then she shifts to a right angle to the student so that she can look directly at him, but the student can choose whether or not to become directly engaged with the worker. Since eye gaze is a powerful means of initiating interaction[10] but also a means for threatening or challenging,[11] the worker's behavior left choices and a space of freedom for the student.

> I entered the ninth-grade classroom and noticed a new student in the class so I sat next to him, placing myself parallel then twisting in my seat so I was positioned at a right angle to him. Thus, he could choose when to have eye contact.

The following instance illustrates the approach-avoidance maneuvering that goes on constantly between workers and clients, often more disguised by the client as he covers up his response. Here, the client is seated on the floor in a mental hospital day room as the worker approaches. The worker, aware that she is looking down on him, and conscious of the extra domination implied in such a position, squats and attempts to meet him intimately, face to face, on the same plane. Failing in this move, she then retreats to a side-by-side, less confronting position at a "casual-personal"[12] distance so that she might pose less threat.

> Mr. Aiken was sitting on the floor of the day room with his knees drawn up to his chest. I bent down in a squatting position directly

<u>in front of him</u>, and said, "Hello." Mr. Aiken immediately cringed and lowered his head. Upon viewing this, <u>I moved to a position alongside Mr. Aiken, leaving about four feet of space between us, and sat down.</u>

Obviously, Mr. Aiken was not ready for this invasion of his personal space, and the worker, grasping his message, controlled her own positioning behavior out of consideration for client comfort.

These illustrations have dealt with social worker behavior intended to consider the comfort of the client. In some instances, however, especially with colleagues or superiors, the worker may adopt positioning behavior expected to generate the opposite of warmth, concern, openness, and nonsuperiority. The following example illustrates such positioning at a staff level. Here, the worker deliberately times her entrance into a staff meeting so that she can sit in the most powerful spot at the table. She is interested in seizing control of the meeting and knows that leadership can best be exerted from the head seat where she can look at everyone at once.[13]

Anticipating a power struggle, <u>I arrived early at the task force meeting in order to occupy the seat at the head of the table.</u>

The final illustration deals with an interaction in which the supervisor is intimidated by the positioning behavior of the worker although he may not be conscious of the source of his vague discomfort. In this instance, it is the worker who exerts the upper hand while she asks the supervisor to be more considerate of staff opinion.

Although many potential clients do not receive service because they work during the day, my supervisor had not been responsive to staff suggestions about keeping the Center open in the evening. Hoping to influence him, <u>I pulled my chair up close to him and faced him directly.</u> As I spoke, <u>I leaned forward and inched my chair further into his space.</u> He leaned backward slightly, rolled his chair back a little (<u>I inched my chair forward more</u>), and said that maybe it's a better idea than he initially thought.

Engaging in the Medium of the Other

To engage in the medium of the other is to parallel what the other is doing, an act which often leads to verbal exchange. This behavior is fitting when its use presumably increases the comfort of the other. For many different reasons (cultural, psychological, age, class, gender, and status variables), some clients may be more comfortable in expressing themselves if approached in other than verbal ways. Sometimes a client is unwilling or uninterested in talking with the worker, perhaps feeling that verbal exchanges put him at a disadvantage.

Children, in particular, are much more communicative through actions than through words and are often able to express themselves more effectively through action or through pieces of verbal exchange "on top of" the action.[14] Often individuals feel most at home when engaged in a medium whose interactional rules are well-known (perhaps guided by ritual, tradition, or prescribed ground rules). Such "first-order communications" may be preferred because they enable the other to recognize easily what he and others are doing, and understand from his own experience the next interactional steps and necessary role performances.[15] In performing known functions, such as making a bed, playing a game, emptying trash, walking, an individual can feel at home and accommodate a social worker who takes part in the act. It is here, then, that certain worker-client interactions must begin. By engaging in the medium of the other, such as doodling next to a doodling individual, digging in the sand with someone who is already digging there, or sitting silently next to a person wrapped in silence, the worker sets the stage for a connection with the client that is necessary in order to work on the task at hand.

In the following illustration the social worker initiates interaction with a young child by joining the activity of interest to him at the moment. Through this parallel behavior, the worker is communicating, "I am interested in you."

During the free play period Bernice, a third-grader, stood all alone looking sad, petting a rabbit in a cage. I too walked over to the rabbit's cage, sat down, and began to pet the rabbit. I waited for Bernice, if she wanted to, to begin to talk with me.

In the next example, the worker notices that her client is reading a magazine. While Mrs. Berry is engaged in her solitary activity, the worker operates with the knowledge that she is the intruder into Mrs. Berry's life space. It is she who is seeking something with Mrs. Berry; Mrs. Berry seems content with her solitary activity. The worker considers where she should position herself vis-à-vis Mrs. Berry, and times her entrance into Mrs. Berry's life carefully by reading her own magazine and sitting for a while nearby before venturing a verbal exchange.

> When I walked into the day room, Mrs. Berry was looking at a magazine. I sat down next to her, picked up a magazine and began to look through it also. Occasionally I would look away from the magazine and I noticed peripherally that when I looked away, she would move the magazine slightly so that she could see me. Finally, she put the magazine down and I did too. I waited a long time (several minutes) before speaking and then I said softly, "Sometimes it's hard to talk." She nodded and looked at the floor.

The stream of life in institutions goes on whether or not the social worker is present. Often, it is the social worker who is perceived as an outsider, both by residents *and* custodial staff, and who must make her entrance into the twenty-four-hour-a-day interactional network with care. In the next instance, the social worker becomes engaged with a client by sharing his silence.

> When Mr. Jory said that the Parole Board said no, he just sat there staring straight ahead of him. I sat down alongside him, leaving about two feet of space between us. For about ten minutes or so we both sat there silently.

There may be no words exchanged, especially when the worker knows that the client's feelings are so powerful that he may want to experience them alone before telling anyone of them at all.

Engaging in the other's medium is a way of connecting to others amply illustrated in the "hanging around" of gang workers and researchers interested in entering the lives of groups when these groups are likely to perceive them as alien at the outset. In the following instance, the social worker wants to give Joe some information obtained from the school counselor about returning to school. Joe is playing with a videogame with James in the Arcade in the shopping mall and is not interested in stopping or in acknowledging the adult who has just approached them. The worker knows it is hard for Joe to talk about his expulsion and his future at that moment, and times his approach with this in mind as he watches the game and then joins them by trying a few games himself.

> When I spotted Joe and James, Joe was engrossed in trying to beat James in a space game at the Video Arcade. I went to their monitor and watched. Joe was the high scorer up to this point. They played three more rounds. I waited and watched, and finally took two turns with him myself. Finally, Joe was out of change. He gave me a long look. I slowly started out of the Arcade and Joe followed me. James started a game with someone else.

Proposing a Medium Presumably Congenial to the Other

To propose a medium presumably congenial to the other is to initiate interaction in a particular activity known by the worker to be familiar to the other. Proposing other than verbal interaction media, like engaging in a nonverbal medium, is used to lead to more open communication when verbal overtures do not bring response or when the worker believes they would not. Again, this behavior is desirable when its use might increase the comfort of the other.

Proposing a medium presumed to be congenial to the other involves making some assumptions about the other's preferred form of interaction. Sometimes the situation suggests a form of interaction other than words, as, for example, taking a walk or playing catch with a child who looks as if talking would not come easily. Or a worker's decision to offer an activity rather than a verbal dialogue might spring from knowledge of age, cultural, or other general characteristics assumed to interest others who seem similar to the person in question. Engaging in an action rather than talking might also be safer for young children, especially in threatening situations.

In certain instances an offer of a cup of tea might break the ice. At other times it is the worker's knowledge about the interests, skills, or accomplishments of the particular person that leads to a specific suggested form of engagement. In order to make such assumptions, the social worker must first reach for analogues. To reach for analogues is to ask the question: "What does this remind me of?" The answer is sought from among the paradigms with which the worker is familiar.[16] By connecting present circumstances with analogues stored in memory, the worker formulates an answer to the professional questions, "What should I do?" "How should I do it?"[17] Based on the particular analogue the worker selects, he offers the client a means through which their interaction can begin that will presumably interest rather than offend. Such proposals of congenial formats are aimed to lead to verbal communication and work on the task that connects the worker and client.

In the following illustration the social worker makes inferences about what a teenager would like to do while talking with him after he notes that she wants to talk with him but is uncomfortable with his office arrangement.

> Kay walked into the office, looked around at all the desks, and frowned at me. I suggested that we walk over to the soda machine.

This example shows the worker deciding upon a form of engagement with a client drawn from generalized knowledge about the likes and dislikes of an age population. To the extent that the worker's knowledge about categories of persons is reliable, he can make such a proposal with confidence. But, as with all categorical knowledge, he must also be prepared for a rejection by any particular individual.

Sometimes, as in the following example, the worker's proposal derives from particular previous experience or knowledge about the individual. Here, the worker knew that Dan liked to play pool and could assume that an offer to play pool with him was a fairly safe suggestion.

> I had spoken to Dan, a patient in the hospital, several times in the recreation area. He usually shot pool during our interactions. Today, he was sitting down, hands clasped over his head, just behind the pool table area. I said, "Hey, want to shoot some pool?"

In the next instance the worker met with Cindy, a four-year-old who had been sexually molested by her father a week before. Mrs.

North brought Cindy to the agency and was tearful and upset, "at my wits end." Cindy was not talking about what happened. She was subdued and ill at ease in the worker's office.

> I had tried to interest Cindy in some of my toys and the sand box. She seemed interested and enjoyed filling a windmill with sand. After several minutes I brought out my male and female dolls and told her it was important for her to touch the dolls the way her daddy had touched her. She glanced at her mother for encouragement and then started to show us what had happened.

The final example of proposing a medium that might be congenial to the other derives from the exigencies of the moment and the social worker's analytic behavior of reaching for an analogue out of his own past. Finding Ed fighting in a school corridor in front of an excited audience, he stopped the fight by physically forcing the student away from the others. Then he took him by the shoulders and walked with him to get rid of the pent-up energy and excitement. The social worker knew that only physical involvement could begin to deal with the heightened physical excitation of the moment. No amount of words would be adequate to the situation.

> After I broke up the fight and the onlookers went to their next class, I noticed that Ed, who had held the other two at bay, was shaking. Remembering my own fights in high school, I thought he might want to walk off some of the left-over feeling, so I led him into an unoccupied room by the shoulders where we walked in large circles while we talked.

Attending

To attend is actively to take in diverse communication cues from the other, and to convey to the other that these are being taken in. Hence, attending behavior involves sensory and cognitive processes on the one hand, and interpersonal communication processes on the other hand. Attending links the inner skills and the interactional skills, for it combines both. Skill in attending refers to the smooth synchroniza-

tion of sensory, cognitive, and communicative processes used continuously during interaction with others regardless of which individual
happens to be speaking at the moment. (In chapter 7 we will describe
scanning, the kind of attending that becomes necessary when meeting with more than one other person.)

In the first place, attending has to do with the processes of perception and cognition. In the perception process the social worker receives various verbal and nonverbal stimuli from the client, screened
and limited by how much of it she is physiologically able to receive.
She then imparts meaning to the messages. That is, she conceptual-
izes them through a translation process in the brain which further
screens and limits how much of the information is taken in through
the grid of her personal/professional frame of reference.[18]

Out of all the stimuli, the social worker decides what is the main
message and what is simply embellishment or distraction, and gears
her attending to encourage expression of the main message. In other
words, between attending and responding to the information or feeling conveyed by client, the social worker uses the cognitive skills that
inform her translation processes: recognizing feelings, looking for
patterns and noting what is missing, drawing inferences, hypothesizing, connecting the new to the old, and reflecting on the work. And
all during these translation processes, the social worker is careful to
separate her feelings and values from those of the client.[19]

To perceive the essence of a situation and to communicate clearly
what one intends to communicate with respect to that situation, one
must not only be aware of one's own values and biases but must be in
control of one's own nonverbal behavior. To refrain from unknowingly
communicating those feelings, attitudes, and judgments which belong within the worker rather than between the worker and the other
requires a particular vigilance on the part of the worker. This is not to
suggest a feeling-less worker nor to propose "scientific objectivity" as
the ideal; for the worker who knows her own feelings and can report
them as needed when working on a given task is the one who can also
encourage the other to know his own feelings as one vital element in
meeting problematic situations.[20] Such sensitivity to the other requires an active internal dialogue through which one's own values,
biases, and feelings at the moment are known as *one's own,* and

controlled in order to maximize perception of the situation and responsiveness to others. That is, it is vital to use the perception skills continuously—looking with planned emptiness, looking at the old as if new, jigsaw puzzling, and looking from diverse angles—in order to attend to the other person with authenticity and accuracy.

Skill in attending appears as seeing and hearing behavior. While the social worker may remain essentially silent during the attending process, she is nevertheless vigorously engaged in an active internal analysis through which she seeks to answer such questions as: What is the other expressing? What is the other *really* expressing? What is he asking of me? Specifically, the social worker is observing the other —his facial expression, posture, gestures, and other bodily cues—by studying his face and the rest of his person through a series of short glances or longer, more intense gazes when messages deemed particularly important are conveyed. She is simultaneously hearing the words themselves and noticing the paralinguistic and emotive aspects of speech—tone, cadence, pauses, pitch, and so forth. In short, the worker is following the other.[21] She is following information and she is following feeling.

At the same time, the worker is also providing a series of tiny communication cues to the other, um-hum, head nods, and so forth,[22] that signal such messages as, "Go on," "I am interested in you," "I am interested in what you are saying." Part of attending is control of the worker's own behaviors so that they are congruent with the message of interest and concern that she wants to convey. For it is patently impossible that the client will feel attended to if the worker is busy jotting down notes, or if she gazes out the window, fidgets, yawns, looks at her watch, or in other subtle (primarily nonverbal) ways transmits a contrary message.[23] To attend, then, is also to convey poised concern that is mobilized in the service of the other.

In the following episode the social worker reveals her own focus upon attending by the detail with which she describes the communication exchange. It is obvious that this worker regards her own behavior as related to, and possibly responsible for, the client's detailed description of her situation. In this example, the worker's "ooh," head nod, tilt of the head, and smile when she detected a bit of sarcasm, are the tiny microacts through which she conveyed her value of Mrs. Frank and encouragement that it would be all right for her to get her complaints off her chest as a prelude to determining just what she wanted the social worker to help with.

> Mrs. Frank came to talk with me about "everything going wrong in the last couple of days." I said, "Ooh" and waited. She continued, "I am married and I have two children, ages five and three. My husband is working as a driver for an electrical company." I nodded. "We moved to the Project two months ago," she went on. "And you know how pleasant it is here," she added sarcastically. I tilted my head a little and smiled. "Well," she said, "it started with the toilet. Then Billy, he's the older one. . . ."

Using the attending skill, the social worker may follow facts or feelings or both. In the example cited, the worker was primarily attending to a factual presentation of the problems the client was facing up to the point where a sarcastic tone suggested the deep feelings that accompanied the facts.

In the next instance, the social worker is attending a flood of feelings expressed by a colleague, a nurse, in a school system. After the nurse is apparently satisfied that the social worker heard her feelings, she moves to present some facts, specific episodes that have given rise to her feelings. In this instance the school nurse is white while the social worker and the students being discussed are black. One can appreciate the strain the social worker must have been under, keeping her own feelings and responses under control as she attended to the other's feelings and biases. Had she not been able to attend to the nurse and really hear her, had she tried to combat these feelings midway through the expression of them, the chances for further work with the nurse would have been diminished.

> While talking with the school nurse about the problems of the pregnant girls in the school, she named some students she would like me to work with and went off into a lengthy description of her opinions about the situation. She detailed her disappointment with those who didn't want abortions, her disgust with their attitude about sex, her opinion of their immaturity, their lack of responsibility, and so forth. I sat quietly and listened and watched as she talked. She then related an episode in which she chastised one girl

with, "Just because you have an abortion doesn't give you a license to engage in sex so freely," and mentioned another who announced in class without any reservation that she was expecting her second child by a second father.

Clearly, this social worker's objectives included hearing out the nurse rather than confronting her opinions and beliefs at that time out of an overreaching desire to make some plan for her own direct involvement with the present students. To reach this end she would have to arrive at a working arrangement with the nurse.

The next episode illustrates the social worker attending a student's presentation of his dilemma and at the same time engaging in an internal analytic process to make sense out of the report she is receiving.

> Talking with John just after the fight he had at school, I said, "Wow, man, you're hot!" and he launched into a description of why this fight had taken place. I listened. From what I could gather this was a gang-related fight. Actually, it was a power-pressure tactic used to recruit him into one of the gangs. He had just been released from the state delinquency institution and thus was a free agent not associated with any gang.

The final episode also illustrates the social worker attending to several aspects at once. In this instance, the multiple demand upon the worker is that of attending to the behavior of several other persons in a group at the same time he is talking to one particular person.

> In a staff meeting of eight persons I reminded Dr. Gamble that he had agreed to distribute the letter to the total staff a week ago. During this interaction Peter was taking notes, and his assistant was frowning. The staff psychiatrist and social services director were looking at Peter and the others were waiting for Dr. Gamble to respond.

These examples of situations suggest that attending is a complex skill. Only on the surface is it simply looking and listening. It is vital to seeing and hearing, and determining what to do next. The worker is taking in cues from the others, and conceptualizing the information she receives. She is concerned about leaving room for the others, and needs to hold her own reactions and ideas in momentary check so that the other gets the impression that he is not following the social worker's scenario, but has really a hand in the course of the interaction. She is also concerned about conveying encouragement and warmth to the client through specific microacts, by smiling, absence of idiosyncratic or distracting movements, frequent eye contact, or a bodily lean toward the client (continued positioning).[24]

4. Skills for Dealing with Feelings

"Consider anything, only don't cry!" Alice could not help laughing at this, even in the midst of her tears. "Can *you* keep from crying by considering things?" she asked. "That's the way it's done," the Queen said with great decision, "nobody can do two things at once, you know."

Lewis Carroll

People have feelings about themselves and their plight, about making decisions, and taking definitive action. People have feelings about having feelings, and all of these are inextricably bound to definition and resolution of the problems they are facing. If the feelings that surround a description of problems, an expression of need, and/or a choice of action are not openly engaged, they become obstacles to the work. They subtly distort information sent and received and/or block movement toward stated goals.[1] Consider the advocates whose clients deny them at the point of confrontation with powerful others. Consider the clients who cannot even begin to think about changing their painful situations until they are satisfied that the essence of their pain has been communicated. Feelings are potent forces in the lives of people,[2] simultaneously pulling them in different directions, skewing their perceptions, hurting and frightening them. If work is to be more than illusory, and problem solving more than a cherished ideal, the worker must deal with feelings.

Basic skills for dealing with feelings include reaching for feelings, waiting out feelings, getting with feelings, talking in the idiom of the other, partializing feelings, reporting own feelings, and containing own feelings. Another skill, reaching for a feeling link, is described and illustrated in chapter 9.

59

Reaching for Feelings

To reach for feelings is to invite the other person to describe the particular emotion or set of emotions that she is experiencing. It is appropriate to do this when one of three conditions obtains: no emotion is expressed in a situation that ordinarily generates emotion; emotion is expressed nonverbally, but not verbally; or emotion expressed seems incongruent with the situation.

Feelings that are frightening, ego-alien, or socially unacceptable are likely to be denied. When such feelings are too potent to be denied, however, they may be expressed nonverbally, through facial expression, posture and gesture, space behavior and/or tone of voice. Silence, too, can be an expression of feeling. At other times feelings are expressed in questions (What's the matter with him?); commands (Don't do that!); accusations (You think you're better than we are); judgments (He's handsome); and sarcastic comments (Another kid: just what I need). In some instances people try to hide what they are really feeling by expressing emotion that is the opposite. Under such conditions, the worker reaches for the feelings of the other by verbalizing the other person's nonverbal behavior in a statement like "You're trembling," or indicating what people usually feel in such a situation with a statement like "That can be exhausting!"[3] Statements are preferable to questions like "What are you feeling right now?" and "How does that make you feel?," because questions place a demand on the other person to produce an answer, a demand which, in and of itself, can disconcert the person, compounding and confounding emotion that is already present.

In the first example, a woman describes a frustrating situation without expressing emotion. The worker reaches for her feelings by describing what is frequently experienced in such a situation.

Mrs. Bond said that she had to work and leave her baby with a sitter, that she wasn't too sure about the sitter but that she couldn't afford a better one. In a very matter-of-fact manner she said that it's okay, though, because she goes home every chance she gets to see how the baby is doing. I said that it must be very frustrating always having to worry about the safety of her child and at the same time

<u>trying to do a good job at work.</u> She sighed deeply, gave me a halfway smile, and said that it was running her ragged.

In the second example the social worker reaches for the feelings of a woman whose expression of emotion is nonverbal by verbalizing the woman's nonverbal behavior.

After a few seconds of silence, Mrs. Taggart said: "My mother can't take care of herself anymore, and my sister wants to put her in a nursing home." Her eyes filled up with tears. <u>"You have tears in your eyes," I said.</u> "I feel guilty about it," she said; "we should be taking care of her."

In the third example, the worker reaches for the feelings of a man whose facial expression seems incongruent with the situation he is describing.

Just before the tenants' meeting, Mr. Vernon told me that the landlord might throw them all out of the building, or get back at them with not enough heat or something like that. He was smiling. <u>I said, "You're smiling."</u> He said, "Yeah? Well I'm a little scared. I've got nowhere else to go."

Waiting Out Feelings

To wait out feelings is to remain silent while the other person experiences her own emotions. This behavior is called for when the worker has just reached for the feelings of the other person, the verbal behavior of the other person stops abruptly, or the nonverbal behavior of the other person seems to signal *time out*.[4]

Waiting out feelings is perhaps the hardest behavior to enact, for silence is discomfiting even when deliberate, and there is a natural tendency to want to fill it with a plethora of words. But people experiencing emotion need room to engage themselves in an internal dialogue through which they can either contact and claim their own feelings, compose themselves in order to project an image of themselves consonant with their preferred self-image, or both. The worker must contain herself lest she deny the other person the right to feel.

In the first example, the social worker reaches for feelings and then silently waits them out.

> The resident in the emergency room called me over to talk with a woman who had been raped a few hours earlier. He said she was so upset they couldn't examine her. I walked into the cubicle where she was sitting on a gurney, shaking all over. <u>"You're trembling,"</u> I <u>said.</u> Then <u>I waited.</u> "It was so awful," she said in a hollow voice. "I'm still so scared." "It <u>is</u> terrifying," I said. I pointed to the blanket lying next to her and asked if she'd like me to fold it so she could put it around her. She nodded.

In the second example, the worker waits out the feelings of an elderly man whose verbal communication stops abruptly. The silence that follows is broken by his active claim to the emotion he is experiencing.

> "Something has to be done about the situation," said Mr. Grey. "I'm not worried about the kids breaking into my place. What worries me is . . ." Silence. <u>I waited.</u> "I'm afraid to walk outside," he whispered.

In the third example, the social worker waits out the feelings of a client whose nonverbal behavior seems to signal *time out*. In this instance, the client follows the silence with an important clue to the possibility that she may be suicidal.

> Ms. Winter said she has an overwhelming fear of being alone and that since her boyfriend moved out four days ago she's been panicky. "That's such a dreadful feeling," I said. "It's worse than you can imagine," she said. I nodded. Then I asked her to describe a little of what about being alone was so scary, and she said, "Sometimes I feel like there's a big, dark . . . emptiness, a kind of void, and I'm just afraid of it." Then she tilted her head up and stared at the ceiling. <u>I waited.</u> After several seconds she said that she was afraid she might jump into it.

Getting with Feelings

To get with feelings is to indicate to the other person that the essence of his inner experience has been communicated and understood. The statement "I understand" will not suffice, for the client has no way of knowing if the worker who says "I understand" actually does understand. Rather, the worker must *demonstrate* her understanding by accurately reflecting the feelings that the client expresses.

In order to get with feelings, then, the worker must put herself in the client's shoes, connect with the client's emotional experience, and offer a congruent statement, like "That *is* painful," or a congruent noise, like "Umph . . . ," when the client says a particular situation was hard to endure. In this way, the worker *shows* the client that she is with him, that she really does understand how it is.

The act of getting with feelings is suitable only when the other person has expressed a feeling or set of feelings in words, and necessary if the client's verbalization of feeling is in response to the worker's reaching for them, or if the client has acknowledged that the feelings for which the worker has reached are in fact the feelings being experienced.

In the first example, the social worker gets with the feelings of the resident supervisor of an institution for children.

> After hanging up the phone, Mrs. Henderson commented that "nobody can do anything by themselves." She told me they constantly bother her. She told me about her many and varied job duties and how tired it all makes her, and how, in addition to all that, she has to make regular rounds, because if she didn't, things were likely to fall apart. I said, "That's exhausting!"

In the second example, the worker initially reaches for feelings, then waits out feelings. The client responds by stating his feelings in words, and the worker gets with his feelings by making a congruent statement.

> Mr. Jackson said he hadn't had any flashbacks for years, that he had gotten help and had learned to control them. "But now it's happen-

ing again," he said; "started last month, and now it's once or twice a day." His hands were tight on the arms of the chair. <u>"You're holding on so tight your knuckles are white," I said.</u> There was a long pause. <u>I waited.</u> "I'm scared to death," he said softly. <u>I nodded.</u> <u>"It is frightening," I said.</u>

In the third example, the worker reaches for feelings, and the client nods, acknowledging that the emotion the worker pinpointed is the one she is experiencing. The worker then gets with the client's feeling by making a congruent noise.

Ms. Richards said that when her welfare check didn't come, she called her caseworker several times, but each time he was out. She said after she lost $1.25 making those calls, she figured she better go down there and see him. "So I walked down there and asked to see him and they told me to have a seat. I waited 4 hours and then another caseworker came out and told me he wouldn't be in today." <u>"That can be so demoralizing!" I said.</u> She pressed her lips together into a thin line and nodded. <u>"Yuk," I said.</u> "Yuk is right," she said.

The flow chart in figure 4.1 depicts the social worker's use of reaching for feelings, waiting out feelings and getting with feelings in the moment-by-moment practice situation. As indicated in the diagram, the key question is, did the client state her/his feelings in words? If the answer is yes, the worker gets with the client's feelings. If the answer is no, the worker reaches for the client's feelings, then asks herself once again, did the client state her/his feelings in words? If now the answer is yes, the worker gets with the client's feelings. If the answer is no, the worker waits out the client's feelings. After several seconds, the worker again asks herself if the client has stated her/his feelings in words. If the answer is yes, the worker gets with the client's feelings. If the answer is no, the worker reaches for the client's feelings again. As a rule, it is appropriate to reach for feelings twice. If, after the second invitation, feelings are neither expressed in words nor acknowledged in a nonverbal form such as a head nod, the social worker is advised to go on. Feelings will manifest themselves many times during an interview, and later attempts to reach for feelings may yet be fruitful.

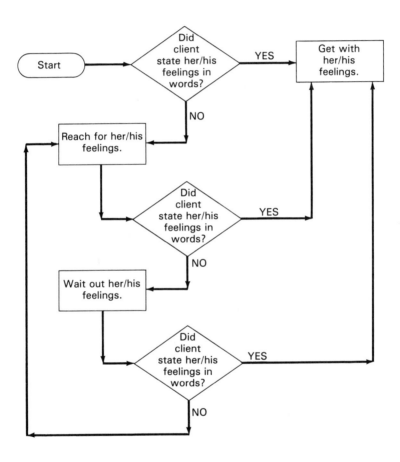

FIGURE 4.1

Talking in the Idiom of the Other

To talk in the idiom of the other is to respond to the other person's disguised, illusory, or veiled messages using the same context and symbols, treating these as if they were real rather than unreal, and as if they were overt rather than covert expressions. By responding in the person's chosen idiom, the social worker does not force the person to expose herself until she is ready, and does not force her to cut off the communication. This behavior is used by the social worker when direct, open communication is not chosen by the client, who, nevertheless, shows a desire to engage with the worker, albeit circuitously. It is a means of keeping the lines of communication open despite the sensitivity of the content.

The assumption underlying use of this behavior is that open communication can be threatening, almost devastating to some persons and to all persons under certain circumstances. For some, discussing problems or even having problems is a sign of weakness that goes against moral values learned elsewhere. To discuss "personal" things with a stranger, the social worker, may seem next to impossible. It is almost as if the person is demeaned by even admitting that she is not fully in command of her situation all of the time and needs outside consultation or help. For others, discussing feelings openly goes against life learnings that are deeply ingrained. In this respect, the American culture has been particularly harsh on men. Many men have learned not to express feelings, often not to feel, lest they be unmanly. Formal education, which has in varying degrees affected the early lives of all persons, has placed value upon thinking, not feeling. Effective thought processes have been rewarded, but little formal teaching is concerned with the feeling or relationship process in school. Any learning in these areas has been a trial-and-error affair, with no grades or medals awarded for success. Moreover, even relatively open people may face certain experiences that seem too unusual, or personal or "crazy" to share with another person. Particularly when shame and guilt take over, people do not relish talking about their concerns. If they do venture into such threatening territory, they may well offer their concerns in an analogy or in terms of "I have a friend who . . ."

Under such circumstances, the social worker talks in the idiom of the other. She regards the client's veiled offering as an opening, not a charade. Later, when it seems possible to do without jeopardizing the beginning rapport, the social worker moves the communication to a more direct and open level.[5]

In the example below, the social worker not only talks in the idiom of the other, she reaches for feelings in the other person's idiom. Then, still in the other person's idiom, she checks to see if the idiom remains necessary.

> After a staff meeting in which the psychologist's plan for a new service was turned down, she asked me if I ever thought about how long it takes a spider to spin a web and how fast it can be wiped out of the corner with a dust rag. I said that it sounded very demoralizing. She looked at me with a sad expression on her face and nodded. I said that spider webs were very vulnerable, and she said that spiders were very vulnerable, too. I nodded. Then I said that sometimes people were vulnerable, giving her a chance to be more direct if she were ready to be. And apparently she was ready, because she said she should never have allowed herself to get so invested in that project.

Partializing Feelings

To partialize feelings is to divide emotional experience into its smaller, more manageable components. This behavior is appropriate when feelings are multiple and/or complex. Partializing feelings is a sorting-out process whereby the social worker helps the client separate the component feelings, one from the other, and attend to each in its turn.[6]

Bereavement, for example, triggers a complex emotional process marked by profound sadness, but including anger, as well, though the anger, often considered unacceptable, may be veiled, dimly felt or totally denied. In addition to sadness and anger, if the loss was of a parent or a partner, the survivor frequently feels abandoned, empty, isolated, lonely, even frightened. Perhaps cheated, too. Such a chaos of emotion can overwhelm the person and inhibit her normal, adaptive responses to the struggle of everyday life. Once each feeling is separated from the emotional whole, recognized, acknowledged, understood, and accepted, however, bewilderment is reduced, leaving the client freer to cope with the event, grieve, and move on.

In the example below, the social worker partializes the feelings of a newly widowed young woman.

> When Mrs. Parsons came into my office, she seemed lost. She walked toward one chair, then another, as if where to sit were an overwhelming decision. I said, "Hi," motioned to one particular chair, and pulled mine closer to it. She sat down where I had designated. <u>"You seem a little discombobulated," I said.</u> "Oh, God, I am," she answered. <u>"That's painful," I said, nodding.</u>

The first thing the worker does is relieve the client's immediate problem of choosing where to sit by pointing to a particular chair. Then the worker reaches for the client's feelings of confusion. When the client acknowledges that she is confused, the worker gets with her feelings, with the pain that confusion evokes. The worker then reaches for information, a skill that is discussed in chapter 5.

> I asked her what lead up to this. "Well," she said, "first Joe died. There was a terrible accident on the expressway and. . . ." Silence. <u>I waited.</u> Her eyes filled with tears. "You're crying," I said softly.

In response to her question, the social worker learns that the woman's husband has died. After appropriately waiting out feelings, she begins to partialize feelings by reaching for the sadness that seems implicit in the woman's tears. Below, the worker continues to partialize feelings by reaching for the anger she thinks she hears in the client's voice, and waits out this feeling. But she does not get with feelings after the client puts her anger in words.

> "That's all I do now," she said. "He left me with two little kids, mortgage payments, and no insurance!" she said angrily. <u>"That can make you angry," I said.</u> There was a long silence during which <u>I waited.</u> "I am angry," she said, "but just because of all the things I have to do that I never counted on. I counted on Joe."

The client, without pausing, has attached her verbalization of anger to a statement that suggests the presence of yet another emotional component of bereavement: a sense of abandonment. So the worker must choose between getting with an already verbalized feeling, anger, and reaching for what may be a newly emergent one, the sense of abandonment. Because the choice arises in the context of partializing feelings, the worker appropriately accords greater weight to the not yet identified feeling that seems to be present. Her aim is to run out the range of different feelings first, knowing it is possible to return to those which seem more troublesome *after* partialization has taken place.

Thus, as can be seen below, instead of getting with the client's anger, the social worker reaches for the feelings of abandonment that may be indicated by the client's statement that she counted on her husband coupled with the unspoken "and now he's not here." The client acknowledges her feelings of abandonment, and the worker gets with them.

> "That can feel like being abandoned," I said. "I do feel abandoned," she said. "Uhmm," I nodded.

The client then puts her anger into words again and verbalizes still another feeling: loneliness. The worker gets with both of these feelings, then reaches for some possible fear that has not yet surfaced. The client confirms the presence of fear, and the worker gets with that feeling as well.

> "And I know it doesn't make sense," she continued; "Joe didn't want to have that accident—but I am angry; and I feel so lonely." "It does make you angry and leaves you very lonely when someone as close as a husband dies," I said. "And it can be scary to face all the things that need to be done right now by yourself." She nodded. "It is frightening," I said.

The worker waits when the client seems to signal "time out"; then, continuing to partialize feelings, she reaches for the sadness the client's face seems to express and waits out the feeling. The client verbalizes a sense of unfairness, and the worker gets with her feelings by nodding.

> Then she closed her eyes. I waited. "God, I miss Joe," she said, with a look of sadness that bordered on despair. "It's unbelievably sad when a husband dies," I said. Then she started to cry. I waited. Her

cries became sobs and she sobbed deeply for several minutes. When she had wiped her face, she looked up and said, "It's not fair. It's not fair." I nodded.

The worker then lists the various components of the client's emotional experience that they have jointly identified, prepares the client for such feelings to continue, and assures the client that they will continue to talk about these feelings in their later meetings.

"We were supposed to have the rest of our lives," she continued. "The children were supposed to grow up with a daddy, not just a mommy." I nodded again. Then I said that we had identified a lot of feelings that she's experiencing: confusion, sadness, anger, loneliness, a sense of abandonment, fear . . . and I said that I imagined she would continue to feel these things for a while and that we'd continue to talk about them in our future sessions.

Reporting Own Feelings

To report one's own feelings is to describe one's own in-the-moment, emotional experience to the other person. This behavior is appropriate only when such self-disclosure is likely to shed light on what the other person is feeling, or what is happening in the situation.

At least two cautions regarding misuse of this behavior should be noted. First, the social worker should not give opinions in the guise of reporting her own feelings. A statement such as "I feel that we are making the decision too quickly," for example, is not a report of feeling. Rather, it is a report of opinion, and is more accurately preceded by "I think"—"I think that we are making the decision too quickly."

Second, the worker should not report her own feelings in order to induce the other person to act. For example, the statement "I feel uncomfortable when you sit there with your coat on" is more than a report of feelings. It is an effort to get the other person to remove his coat. The worker reports her own feelings not to tell others how to behave, but to make her feelings available as information that others can use, if they wish and as they wish, in order to contact their own feelings and/or understand the dynamics of the situation.

In the first example, the worker reports her own feelings to a group of high school students and their parents in order to shed light on what others may be feeling when the atmosphere of a meeting dramatically changes after one student's remark.

> The group was engaging in a final rehearsal before the meeting with school administrators. Mr. Sloane made his extreme demand in a loud voice and Mrs. Neff qualified it, as planned. Mr. Tubman, who was playing the role of principal, said that he understood the parents' concern and supported it, but that the parents would have to understand that the schools can't raise a child's God-given intelligence level. Suddenly Ronald shouted, "You racist bastard!" In the moments that followed there was some laughter and a lot of chattering. The role playing stopped, and, although both students and parents continued to discuss the impending meeting, the interaction was very strained. <u>I said that I felt tense and wondered if anyone else felt that way too.</u>

In the second example, the social worker reports her feeling of defensiveness to a group of staff people in order to shed light on what may be happening in that situation, i.e., an attack.

> Following my comment that we sometimes see crazy behavior because this is a mental hospital and we expect and look for crazy behavior, one of the psychiatrists asked me if I knew much about pathology. I felt my muscles tense up and <u>I said, "Wow! I'm starting to feel defensive!"</u>

Containing Own Feelings

To contain one's own feelings is actively to inhibit expression of one's emotional responses. This is the opposite of reporting feelings. It is appropriate whenever the worker experiences feelings which would neither help the client to contact his own feelings, nor shed light on what is happening in the situation.

Sometimes a client's description of his experience stirs up feelings in the worker. Perhaps the worker was once in a similar situation. Perhaps the client's narration of instances of ill-treatment he was forced to endure fires up the worker's anger and sense of outrage. These emotions should be contained so that they do not interfere with the client's own thinking-feeling process. Mutual self-disclosure, such as in friendship, is eschewed in a professional social worker–client relationship.

This is not to suggest that social workers refrain from stating their opinions regarding the right of all human beings to be treated with dignity and to be protected from abuse by violent others, whether these others be parents, partners, or strangers. Such opinions should be stated as opinions, however. Opinions are a special and important form of information that will be discussed further in chapter 5.

In the example below, the social worker properly contains intense emotions evoked in her by the client's story.

> With wide, frightened eyes and her hands clasped tightly together, Mrs. Willis said that her husband bashed their four-year-old in the face with his fist, kicked her repeatedly, then threw her down the stairs. I tried to keep my face from registering the horror I felt. My stomach turned over and I could feel nausea rising up. I swallowed hard to keep my feelings in check so that I could reach for her feelings. I said in a soft voice, "It can be terrifying to see that happen." She burst into high-pitched sobs.

5. Skills for Dealing with Information

'Twas brillig, and the slithy toves
    Did gyre and gimble in the wabe;
All mimsy were the borogoves,
    And the mome raths outgrabe.

Lewis Carroll

Information is a resource that reduces uncertainty by giving form or character to a situation or event. A situation or event is knowable to the extent that information pertinent to that situation or event can be generated, collected, manipulated, and reconstructed. And to the extent that a situation or event is known, there can be greater accuracy in problem definition and determination of action to resolve the problem defined. It follows that generating and processing information is central to social work practice.

Basic skills for dealing with information include reaching for information, partializing, giving feedback, confronting distortion, checking out inferences, connecting discrete events, recasting problems, giving information, universalizing, running out alternatives, pointing to possible consequences, and summarizing.

Reaching for Information

To reach for information is to ask the other person for facts, opinions, impressions, or judgments that increase knowledge of a situation or event. This behavior should be used when the nature of a situation or event is uncertain. It should be noted that this precludes worker efforts to elicit already known information in order to teach or otherwise influence (Socratic method) the other person.

Questions that reach for information can be open-ended or close-ended.[1] An open-ended question is one that cannot be adequately answered with one or two words. Rather, it seeks description or elaboration. Questions like "What happened?" and "What led up to . . . ?" are open-ended. Such questions are useful for exploring events with the client.[2] When particular details of a situation are unknown or unclear, close-ended questions are important. A close-ended question is one that can be adequately answered with one or two words. Yes-or-no questions are close-ended, for example.

Questions that begin with the word *what* are preferable to those that begin with the word *why*. *What* questions ask for description and as such, are less threatening than *why* questions, which seem to ask for justification. In general, *why* questions can be converted into *what* questions with relative ease, so that worker efforts to obtain necessary information are enhanced, rather than hampered by this semantic shift.

In the example below, a social worker at a substance abuse center reaches for information, using an open-ended question to explore. The client's response stops abruptly, so the worker appropriately waits out her feelings. After the silence, the client provides the information which the worker reached for.

> Mrs. Benson said that she had done it again. "Done what?" I asked. "Did myself in again," she said; "I went out Friday night and. . . ." Silence. I waited. After several seconds she said, angrily, "I got drunk. I stayed dry for eighty-three days—eighty-three days! Then in one night, I blew it!" "That can make you feel angry and sad and just awful," I said. She started to cry.

Later in the same session, Mrs. Benson talks about some of what makes it hard for her to stay dry. After the worker reaches for her feelings and Mrs. Benson indicates what she really feels, she refers to a person whose identity is unclear to the worker. So the worker reaches for information with a close-ended question to clarify.

> ". . . and when I get upset, I want to talk to my husband about it. But every time I try to talk to him about what's going on with me, he says he's tired of my pain and why don't I just go drown my troubles in a bottle like I used to." "That can really hurt," I said. "No," she said; "it just pisses me off. What hurts is when she says it." "Who?" I asked. "My daughter," she replied.

Partializing

To partialize is to divide a problem into smaller, more manageable parts. This behavior is appropriate when the pressures that the client describes are many and complex or when simultaneous concern with many aspects of a problem confounds the work.

People confronted by large and complex problems tend to feel them as total life experiences that cannot be altered. Such statements as "Everything is wrong" and "There is nothing that can be done" reflect a totality that both overwhelms and immobilizes. Likewise, the many complex issues that can arise in the course of selecting action to accomplish a task can diffuse energy and retard progress toward the goal. By partializing, the social worker separates the overwhelming whole into a series of manageable units.

In the example below, the worker gets with the felt totality that the client's initial statement reflects, reaches for information with an open-ended question to explore the situation, and then partializes the pressures impinging on the client into two separate units for action.

> Mr. Brecker said that everything suddenly collapsed. "Wow!" I said. "What happened?" He said that two months ago he was working and looking forward to retiring so he and his wife could do some of the things they always talked about doing. Now nothing. He went on to describe his wife's death and his futile efforts to keep the company from retiring him. He said there was nothing to do, nobody to be with, and no reason to get up in the morning. After we talked about how lonely he feels <u>I said that two things seemed to be making him feel lonely: not having anything to do since he didn't have a job, and not having anyone to be with since his wife died.</u>

Giving Feedback

To give feedback is to repeat the essence of what the other person has said and ask if the meaning received was, in fact, the intended meaning. It is appropriate for the social worker to give feedback whenever she thinks or even suspects that she has not really understood what the client is trying to convey. The worker uses this behavior to increase her accuracy in recognizing meaning.[3]

Feedback is necessary to expose distortions in the specific content of a message. A message may have come across garbled, vague, in unfamiliar words, or incomprehensibly circuitousness. In such instances the social worker paraphrases what she thinks she heard by stating in her own words what the other person's remark conveyed to her. The paraphrase is an at-the-moment, descriptive statement that aims to clarify the communication by involving the other person in actively listening to the receiver's version of what he said. This version is then either confirmed or rejected as inaccurate with respect to the meaning intended; and, if rejected, the other person can then correct his statement or otherwise adjust his presentation to be more accurate.

In the following example, it is through giving feedback that the social worker at a day center for homeless people begins to understand the plight her client is trying to describe.

As soon as I arrived, a young woman who introduced herself as Cindy said, "They won't give me food stamps. I knew they didn't like me when I was down there. I got an address for them to send it to and everything. You know, they have stuff on there that you just can't answer. How many people live with you at that address? How many of them get food stamps? I didn't write nothing on them lines. I don't live nowhere. And I don't have nothing. That's why I need food stamps. I gotta eat." I said, "Let's see if I got this: You filled out a form for food stamps but you left some lines blank because you don't have a place where you live. Is that right?" "Yeah," she said. "But you did give them an address; is that right?," I asked. "Yeah," she said, "a social worker at one of the shelters got me a post office box." "Oh," I said, "that's why you can't answer a question like how many people live with you at that address!" "Yeah," she said. "Now what's this about them not liking you?" I asked. "Well they didn't send me no food stamps," she said.

In the next example, the social worker at Cross Springs Retirement Home gives feedback and learns that the meaning he took from an elderly woman's statement was very different from what she intended to convey. And in this instance, that difference makes a big difference in the direction that the social worker needs to go to alleviate her plight.

> "... and I miss my bottom teeth," she said. "Sometimes I only eat the soup—the clear part. The rest of the food, if I swallow without chewing it up, I'll get sick." <u>"Are you telling me you lost your false teeth here in the building?" I asked.</u> "No. No," she said. "I never had false teeth."

Confronting Distortion

Like giving feedback, confronting distortion is aimed at increasing accuracy in communication of consequential information. The social worker gives feedback in an effort to correct her own inaccuracies, and confronts distortion in an effort to correct inaccuracies on the part of the other person.

Thus, to confront distortion is to present information that counters inaccuracies by the other person. This behavior is appropriate when information provided by the other person is partial, skewed, or otherwise inaccurate; or when the other person's verbal and nonverbal expressions of feeling are contradictory.

Because people view the world through the filter of their past experience, their values, beliefs, and current concerns, they do not use all the information about the world of people and events that their senses are able to receive. Moreover, because people anticipate the reactions of others and attempt to project particular images of themselves and their situations at different times, they sometimes present only a selective piece of the already selective information they have received. In addition, wishful thinking, fear of exposure, and efforts to induce others to respond in certain preferred ways further combine to distort information presented. Such distortions can block work on tasks by preventing discussion of relevant concerns and/or precluding a range of choices that the client could consider in selecting action to decrease the pressures impinging on him. Therefore, the worker confronts distortion.

In the first example, a social worker at a spouse abuse center confronts a man who assaulted his wife with his distortion of what he actually did to her.

"I'm sorry, for chrissake," the guy said to me. "Look, Jack," he continued, "I just slapped her around a little." "No," I said, "that's not true. You blackened her eye and dislocated her jaw."

In the next example, the social worker confronts distortion when a man's nonverbal expression disclaims the validity of his verbal expression.

Mr. Seymour said that everything was all right, but his facial muscles were tense and his expression was troubled. I told Mr. Seymour that by the look on his face, everything was not all right. Then Mr. Seymour nodded and said that he was just making it.

Checking Out Inferences

To check out an inference is to ask if a certain thought, hunch, or interpretation is valid for the other person in a particular situation. Inferences are important because they often offer the client new insights and connections the client missed from her position inside of an experience.[4] But they can be dangerous, too. As indicated in chapter 1, inferences are, by definition, statements that have not yet been confirmed or disconfirmed. Thus they are not sufficient bases for action until they have been checked out and confirmed. It is necessary to check out inferences whenever inferences are drawn.

The social worker can check out an inference by stating the inference and then asking the client if the statement is accurate. Even if the worker strongly believes that his inference is accurate, if the client disconfirms it, it is not useful at that time in that situation.

In the example below, the social worker at the juvenile detention center checks out an inference that suggests the boundary of a problem may have been drawn too narrowly in the past. The client is a twelve-year-old- boy whose parents filed a third complaint against him for stealing in less than six months.

I asked Shawn if he took the money and he said, "Yeah, I took it. It was there and he knew I was broke. He should have moved it. Now I'm in trouble with the whole family, not just him and you people."

"Who's he?" I asked. "My old man," he said; "he knew I'd take it. He should have moved it." "Sounds like you think he set you up, right?" I said. "Yeah; he likes to pull that kind of stuff," Shawn replied.

In the following example, the social worker checks out an inference, reaches for information with an open-ended question, checks out another inference, then reaches for feelings.

Mrs. Chambers came in with puffy eyes. "You've been crying, right?" I said. "Right," she said, "and I'd still be crying if there were any tears left in me." "What happened?" I asked. "We just got the results of my husband's blood test back," she said. "Bad, right?" I said. "Right," she said. "He has herpes. That means I probably have it too." "That can be devastating!" I said. "That Goddamn sonovabitch! That Goddam sonovabitch!" she yelled.

In the next example, the social worker draws and checks out an inference regarding the basis of a young mother's anxiety. The worker attends while the mother talks, reaches for the mother's feelings, then checks out her inference.

Mrs. Keenley came in to see me before the group meeting. She said that even though the group agreed not to bring their children with them to the meeting, she was afraid to leave Kenny with a sitter. She cuddled him and said as if thinking aloud to herself, "I don't know what I'd do if something happened to him!" Then she looked directly at me and said, You know, Ms. McBride, when he was sick, I carried him to the hospital every other day, and even to a private doctor." I nodded. "He's so little," she continued, "I don't think anyone else would take up as much time with him as I do." She smiled down at him and kissed him. Then her face became long, she glanced my way without turning her head, then started speaking very slowly. "My first baby died when she was only three months old. The doctor told me that she had a fifty-fifty chance, and then three days later she was dead." "Oh, how awful!" I said; "that must have been really rough on you." She agreed and added, "Yeah; that's why I'm afraid to leave Kenny with anyone. Everytime he gets sick—even with a cold—I rush him to the hospital." "Mrs. Keenley," I asked, "are you afraid that Kenny will suddenly get sick and die, too?" She nodded. After a brief silence she said, "You can never tell with babies."

Connecting Discrete Events

To connect discrete events is to ask the other person if two or more separate occurrences may be related. This behavior is suitable when clients do not connect the events they describe if the social worker infers a connection, and if connecting the events puts a different perspective on the situation. With respect to the first condition, connecting discrete events can be understood as a special case of checking out inferences. In terms of the second condition, connecting discrete events is related to recasting problems, a skill discussed later in this chapter.

The number and complexity of interaction sequences in the various systems of demand and relationship in which persons live their daily lives can obscure connections between events so that each seems self-contained and wholly separate from the others. Similarly, political and economic events can seem unrelated to interpersonal relations and inner experiences. By connecting apparently discrete events, problems can be understood from new perspectives; pressures can be seen to emanate from different sources; and new actions to lessen the pressures can be taken.

In the example below, the social worker's connection of discrete events enables a middle-aged man to begin to understand in a new way the series of social rejections that had mystified and depressed him over the years. The social worker listens to the man's story, reaches for information, checks out an inference, then connects discrete events.

> Lewis, a forty-eight-year-old lawyer, came for treatment of depression, his almost constant companion since he left his wife five years ago. He said he did have two "up" periods, about two-and-a-half months each, separated by three years. Both "up" periods began with what he called "meaningful" relationships with young, intelligent women. The first was Judy, and he saw her less than a week

when she told him she couldn't see him anymore—that she was tired. Lewis said he laughed, told her he hadn't meant to keep her out so late, and that she should get a few good nights of sleep and he'd see her the following week. But she said no, that she didn't want to see him again. He asked her what he had done wrong, and she said nothing, that he was a nice guy but that he was too much for her. With great passion, he described the next few months when all he could think of was how to get her to understand him so she'd see him again. He called her many times, at home and at work, and sent her many letters. She did not respond.

Two years later he met Jane who told him after one dinner date that he wants too much. He didn't understand. She hadn't even invited him in for coffee when he took her home. Again he phoned and wrote letters, but to no avail. Again he felt deeply rejected.

From what he told me and from the urgent way he spoke about everything in our sessions, and stared at me when he spoke, I began to think a major problem could be his intensity—good in the courtroom, but often draining in one-to-one, undiffused social situations. It seemed like he felt most "up" when he was intensely involved with another person, but with this very intensity, he was depleting their energy and they were distancing him in self-defense. If I were on the right track, my hypothesis should hold for relationships with men as well as women, so I asked him if he had any close male friends. He said no, then told me one of the saddest moments in his life was when he was spending a week in Chicago on business and his old college roommate couldn't find any time to get together with him, not even for some small talk over a quick breakfast. "But you don't really make small talk, do you," I said. "No, I don't," he agreed. "Do you think your intensity has anything to do with the two women and your college buddy not wanting to spend time with you?" I asked. "My intensity," he repeated. "Yeah," I said; "all the energy you put out and kind of demand that they put out, too." Then there was a long silence. Finally, after two or three minutes, he said, "You know, I've lost a lot of friends over the years, and I've been told enough . . . enough." Another silence.

Recasting Problems

Like connecting discrete events, recasting problems is done in order
to put a new perspective on events. More specifically, to recast a
problem is to provide a different vantage point for thinking about
troublesome issues, thereby shifting and/or increasing the range of
alternative actions considered appropriate for dealing with them.[5] This
skill should be used whenever the client seems stuck with one definition of the problem under discussion, the client's one definition is not
the only way to frame the problem, and the client's definition is
deleterious to herself or hinders potential problem resolution.

In the following example, a child protective services social worker
recasts the problem for a child who has been sexually assaulted and
blames herself for it.

> After talking and playing with the anatomically correct dolls for a
> while, five-year-old Jennie told me that when her daddy bathes her,
> he gets in the tub with her, puts her on his lap, and pokes her pee-
> pee with his hotdog. She picked up the little girl doll and banged its
> head on the floor. I said, "Jennie, you didn't do anything bad." I
> picked up the daddy doll and compared it to the little girl doll.
> "Look," I said, "Daddy is a lot bigger than you. You were too little to
> make him stop." Then I cuddled the little girl doll and said, "The
> little girl wasn't bad. The big daddy was bad." She looked up at me
> with big eyes. "You're a good little girl," I said. She reached for my
> hand.

In the second example, a social worker recasts a problem encountered by a group of elderly people.   .

> One of the senior citizens began writing a list of those present
> and their phone numbers. Several people had difficulty recalling
> their numbers and seemed embarrassed by it. Someone said, "That's
> what happens when you get old." Others agreed. I said that some-
> times I have trouble thinking of my phone number simply because
> I never call myself on the phone. One woman said that she remem-
> bers other people's numbers but not her own. Another woman said
> they should be careful before they blame everything on being old.

Several people helped each other by one reminding another of his phone number.

Giving Information

To give information is to offer the other person facts, opinions, or ideas that may increase that person's knowledge of a situation or event. This behavior is appropriate only when the information is relevant to the task at hand and not already available to the other person.

As indicated at the beginning of the chapter, information is a resource. Given the relationship between possession of resources and possession of power, when the worker gives the client information, she increases the client's power to exercise some measure of control over his own experiences.[6] But this proposition holds only when the information is both relevant and not previously available to the client. Giving information that is not relevant diverts attention from the situation at hand, and giving information that the client already has tends to influence the client's decision by emphasizing particular facts or opinions. In both instances the client's power to make decisions in accord with his own definition of his best interests in a particular situation is decreased rather than increased.

A third, related caution should be noted. Ideas and opinions that are presented as "truths" distort and manipulate, decreasing the client's power to determine the course of his own life. For the client's power to be increased by the ideas and opinions that the worker offers, the worker must present them as her own and indicate that other people may have different opinions.

In the first example, the social worker gives information that serves to relieve some of the distress a young man is experiencing in the aftermath of a rape. The worker listens, waits out feelings, and then gives information.

Mr. Palmer said they jumped him when he was jogging, that he always jogged about 5 a.m. and he was never scared. He said he never even gave it a thought that something like that could happen. He also said he never worried about his mental health before, but now he can't stop crying when he thinks about it, which is most of the time. Then there was a very long silence. I waited. Mr. Palmer stared at his shoes for a few seconds, then looked past me out the window and said, "I had an orgasm." "Do you know that's not unusual when a man gets raped?" I asked. His eyes met mine. "It's not unusual?" he asked. "No, it's not," I said. He sighed and his shoulders dropped down like he was relieved.

In the second example, the social worker gives factual information, and then information of the opinion type. In the latter instance, she explicitly defines the opinion as her own.

Mrs. Howard asked me how to get to Third and Arcady and I told her which bus went there. She told me she didn't have money for the bus, that she wanted to know how to walk there. I told her how and then said that I thought it was dangerous for a woman to walk there alone at night, that other people might not agree, but that it seemed dangerous to me.

Universalizing

Universalizing is a special case of giving information. It is intended to connect people with their common humanity and offer them hope when they are struggling with difficult situations that are part of the human condition. The message to the client is that her experience is not only painful and real, it is also universal. Others have been there and others will be there. One can neither avoid it nor ignore it. It must be endured until the pain eases. Because others have been there, we know that it can be endured and that it will ease, even if, at the moment, it seems intolerable and eternal.

It should be noted that universalizing is different from generalizing. Generalizing takes the client's experience to a level of abstraction that can minimize it and suggest to the client that, because others have had a similar experience, her experience is no big deal. In universalizing, quite the opposite is true. Experience is deepened and enriched by the connection to fellow sufferers. The fear that one's feelings are strange is alleviated. The suggestion is that the client is "in the same boat" as all other human beings, stuck with her humanity and the painful price of it.

In the following example, the social worker gets with feelings, then universalizes.

After learning that her elderly mother suffered a stroke, Carla told me that she was frightened. She said that her mother would probably not live much longer, and that even though she rarely sees her, she knows she's out there; that because of that, in a way, she's never really alone. She said she knew she'd be sad when her mother dies, but she didn't realize she'd feel scared and alone. I nodded. "Life is never the same after a mother dies," I said, "never the same again."

Running Out Alternatives

Like universalizing, running out alternatives is a special case of giving information. In this instance the information is intended to provide the other person with the greatest number of possible options for dealing with the problems being faced.

To run out alternatives is to list possible courses of action for the other person to consider.[7] Use of the behavior is illustrated in the following example, where a social worker at a prison gives information, reaches for information, then runs out alternatives for a new inmate.

Ray said that Grayson (cell mate) told him the worst thing you can do in here is nothing, that you stay in your cell except for fifteen minutes at mealtimes and a recreation period. "Is that true?" he asked me. "It's true," I said. "He said the best jobs are kitchen and library," Ray continued. "I guess they're all taken, aren't they?" he asked. "Yeah, they are," I told him, "but there are openings in other areas like shoe repair, building maintenance, the dispensary." I paused, but Ray didn't say anything more. So I asked him if he knew we had education and training programs here. "I'm not illiterate," he snapped. I told him I knew that, that I saw he got A's in high school English and math and a B+ average. "I meant college. You can do a two-year associate's degree or even a full four-year bachelor's degree in either business or sociology. Or," I went on, "we have programs in auto mechanics, barbering and printing." "I can go to college in here?," Ray asked, looking surprised. "You sure can," I said.

Pointing Out Possible Consequences

To point out possible consequences is to indicate the possible outcomes of actions under consideration by the other person. As the two examples of this behavior illustrate, it is frequently, though not always, used in combination with running out alternatives.

Like universalizing and running out alternatives, pointing out possible consequences is also a special case of giving information and is therefore subject to the conditions for giving information. The social worker points out only those consequences that are relevant and that presumably have not been already considered by the client.

In the first example, the social worker at a high school reaches for feelings, gets with feelings, then points out some of the possible consequences of a student's plan of action.

Danny said he was going to drop out when he turned sixteen. He said his classes were piss poor and boring and the ridiculous homework assignments took too much time away from his art work. He said he still planned on college as an art major, that, in fact, by dropping out he'd have two years to work and earn his tuition. He said he'd take the General Education Degree when he was eighteen, do nothing but draw and paint that summer, and start college in the fall. "It's hard to keep going to school when classes don't meet your expectations," I said. "It's the pits," he said. "It is tough," I said. "And there are consequences to your alternative plan, too," I said. "First, you'll have to wait three years, not two, before you can take the GED. The rule is one year after your class graduates. Second, you'll miss out on scholarships, and two of them are for art alone. And third, for those three years that you won't have a high school diploma, you probably won't be able to earn more than minimum wage."

In the second example, the social worker runs out three alternatives and points to a possible consequence.

Mr. DeAngelo said that he couldn't bear the thought of spending the rest of his life in a nursing home. He said that there was nothing to do there, and that most of the residents were senile, and that he feared for his own sanity. After much discussion during which he expressed a lot of feeling and I tried to get with the feelings he was expressing, he asked me what he could do. I said that there were at least three alternatives we could explore. There are other nursing homes; there are boarding homes; and there is the possibility of living with a relative, if that was okay with him and with the relative. He said that relatives were out, but that a boarding home or even a different nursing home might make a difference. He said it certainly couldn't be worse than it was here. I said that other nursing homes might also have residents who were senile. He nodded and said he could take that if there were something to do, or if there were nothing to do but not all that senility—he just couldn't take both at the same time.

Summarizing

To summarize is to state the essence of a particular discussion or series of discussions, action or series of actions. This behavior is indicated whenever next steps are to be determined. It should be used at the end of a transaction in order to specify the issue for a future interaction and/or the actions to be taken in the interim. It should be used at the beginning of a transaction in order to set the focus. And it can be used to refocus people whose talk has strayed from the task at hand.[8]

Summarizing answers the question, Where have we been? Therefore its use should precede efforts to answer the question, Where do we go from here?

In the example below, the social worker summarizes at the beginning of a session in order to set the focus.

Mrs. Black and I greeted each other. Then I said, "Last week we talked about your son's difficulties in school. It was difficult for you. I know, because you were very upset about his poor performance after he had done so well in school before. We decided that you would set aside some time to talk to your son and we went over some things you could say to him. We also decided you would set up a meeting with his teacher. You were nervous about that, but you felt you should do it. This week you were going to tell me how the meetings went."

PART THREE

Skills for Working with Groups

6. About Groups

Everyone has a place, is embedded in nourishing relationships, perceives order and meaning, and is relatively unselfconscious.

Philip Slater

A 1985 NASW report on the effectiveness of social work practice in mental health programs analyzed 142 studies and found *the use of group process* the third most frequently used among 26 "intervention techniques."[1] Yet, the particulars of group work are all too often overlooked as social workers learn and refine their approach to clients, which ordinarily favors a one-to-one orientation.

Practitioners from other disciplines and group "facilitators" often say they *run* groups. When they speak of working with individuals, they do not speak of running individuals! Yet they run groups. Such a curious vocabulary says something about subtle, professional-technical, elitist orientations, and thus about the control issues involved in treating or facilitating groups. Some workers say they lead groups and call themselves "leaders," thus eliminating a major dynamic to be developed within the group: the emergence of leadership! These "leaders" may be either controlling or passive; they have not learned enough about group processes and group-focused skills to find their place *within* the group. They may either dominate or say virtually nothing (also a subtle means of control). In any case, the particular skills for working with groups *from within the group process* may be unknown or not valued. The stance of these workers seems to be superimposed upon the group rather than being an inherent part of it.

The usual focus of many practitioners is upon dealing with individuals who happen to be in a group. It is not on the group itself. The group is seen only as context for the work with individuals. In other words, group work is simply work with grouped individuals. It is group-oblivious work.

The self-help group literature suggests a facilitative or consultative stance for the professional.[2] But it deals more with programmatic and organizational matters than worker behaviors within the group process. Feminist group literature proposes an egalitarian worker posture and an emphasis upon collaborative group process.[3] Perhaps a contribution toward articulating a group-focused practice will come from this arena.

As we see it, social workers *do not* run groups. They help groups to organize, develop, and run themselves. They help the participants to develop a system of mutual aid. We aim to highlight the skills for doing this in chapters 7, 8, 9, and 10.

Elsewhere, we have described social work with groups as a group-focused approach.[4] The individuals remain a critical concern of the practitioner, but develop and achieve their goals through attention to the group itself. In such an approach, the practitioner gradually helps the group participants take control of their group life.

We shall identify in this section certain special skills that enable social workers to adopt such a stance—a stance focused on enhancing the groupness of groups. These skills are additional to all the skills we have described in chapters 1 through 5. They augment the skills used in working with individuals. There will remain always the need for dealing with each group participant, but there are special intentional behaviors for those who wish to notice and deal with the groupness of the group and who see this as a powerful way to affect individuals.

This orientation assumes that groups are entities with many helpers, not simply with the worker or co-leaders as central influencers. The social worker, a power-sharer, gives away her power. And as the group assumes increased responsibility for its direction(s), the worker encourages this empowerment.

There is a choice in practice with groups as to the level of intervention the worker will pursue. She may focus a response at an intrapersonal or interpersonal or group level. Let us illustrate this point.

Jane glares at Jim during a heated group discussion and says, "Whenever anyone in this group comes up with a plan, others have a yes-but response." On the intrapersonal level the worker can say to Jane, "That can make you angry," then wait. Or on the interpersonal level the worker can say, "Jim, do you know what Jane is angry with you about?" Or on the group level, <u>reaching for a feeling link,</u> the worker can say, "Does anyone else feel the way Jane is feeling?"

Our focus will be on skills for group-level responses.

We realize there are types of groups and certain times in any group experience where the practitioner is the teller, the treater, the instructor. And there are multitudes of books and resources that describe these approaches. We will limit our attention here to skills aimed to help the *group* be the major source of influence, with hopes that group-conscious workers may then have more of an informed choice about the stance they will assume in their group work. We also shall identify situations where the group does *not* sieze the initiative after the worker makes a group-focused move, and we will show how to attend to the involved individual in such an instance.

APPLICABILITY OF GROUP-FOCUSED SKILLS

So far, we have referred to the worker and to the leadership role in considering the use of group-focused skills. But these skills and behaviors are far more versatile than just being useful to the central person. They can be used by any of the group participants as well. In our experience we have stressed the versatility of group-focused skills for all persons in the group as ways to enhance group performance from the side-lines. And we have found that much positive change in group functioning can be accomplished by a group participant who deliberately tries to affect the group process from where he is.

It seems important to mention here that much of the social worker's time and energy will be spent in groups—in staff meetings, case conferences, treatment planning, and so forth. The use of the group skills, which we shall elaborate in chapters 7 through 10, will help improve the quality of the group experience from the inside-out, so to speak.

While we shall be using the term "group skills," we must add that the reader should think of them also as "team skills." Thinking of these as team skills not only emphasizes their importance, since so much of the worker's time is spent in teams and meetings with colleagues and other workers (often in boring, ineffective meetings), but accents their special importance for social workers since they occupy a particular place in team meetings, especially interdisciplinary ones. Effective teamwork helps social workers make and effect comprehensive and coordinated treatment and discharge plans. Research has shown that social work team members are more likely than other members to take active roles in helping the interdisciplinary team function effectively.[5]

USING INDIVIDUAL-FOCUSED SKILLS IN THE GROUP

When one moves to working with a group, it is not like entering a totally foreign land. The social worker will still use the skills described for individual work, for these are basic. There will be some differences. For example, the "attending" skill we have described will now be called "scanning" since the worker will "attend" to many, not merely one person at a time. We will come back to scanning in chapter 7. The worker will also use the other "stage setting" skills (chapter 3): tone setting, positioning, engaging in the medium of the other, and proposing a medium congenial to the other, since these are equally applicable to group situations.

The "perception" and "cognitive" skills still pertain, but are extended to encompass the total group complexion. In the realm of the "skills for dealing with feelings" you will not first reach for, wait out, and get with individuals' feelings in an emotion-laden situation without using group-focused skills, e.g., reaching for a feeling link, amplifying subtle messages, and softening strong messages. And as the social worker accents group-conscious communications in the verbal as well as the nonverbal realm, she will continue to use all the "skills for dealing with information" described in chapter 5. But she will, in addition, need to reach for an information link, redirect a message, suggest communication patterns, and employ other group-focused skills geared to building the group and facilitating the work of the participants. These group focused skills will be described in chapters 8 and 9.

In chapter 7 we consider skills that can occur only in situations of more than two persons, i.e., more than the social worker and client. All of the skills identified in chapters 7, 8, 9, and 10 will presume that this condition applies. Chapter 7 concerns those skills which the social worker uses continuously in the group in contrast to the other skills which will be used in particular instances. We refer to these as the "continuous group skills." Chapters 8 and 9 focus on the "contingent group skills," those used only when certain conditions signal their use. In chapter 8 we deal with "skills for buildings groups." Chapter 9 concerns a different focus, "skills for facilitating the work of the group." In chapter 10 we examine "skills for non-talking groups" and "non-talking times with groups." Here we look at situations where the talk arises out of a shared activity, action, or chore.

7. Continuous Group Skills

> Invisible rhythms underlie most of what we assume to be constant
> in ourselves and the world around us. Life is in continual flux.
>
> Gay Gaer Luce

As we turn to consider the group-focused skills, we shall follow the same approach we have taken with the individual-focused skills. We shall offer a definition of the skill area and then define each skill within that area as it is identified. Following this, we describe *when* the skill is employed, i.e., the condition(s) that signal its use, the *how* of the skill (the action that conveys this skill), and finally *what it looks like* in a practice vignette.

We have identified three skills as "continuous group skills"; i.e., they are skills that need no particular impetus to signal their use. They must be used all the time, every moment you are in a group situation. They are probably the most uniquely *group* skills among all of the skills for working with groups. Clearly, they are at the heart of the difference between workers who appreciate the groupness of groups and those whom we have called group-oblivious workers.

The three continuous skills are: thinking group, scanning, and fostering cohesion. We shall consider each of these in turn as critical driving forces for group work.

Thinking Group

Thinking group is having group concepts as a mind-set, a frame of reference for looking at and making sense of what is happening in the group.[1] It is a cognitive skill. Thinking group implies that group concepts take precedence over individual or personality concepts and dynamics as a glass through which the worker "sees" what is going on. The social worker uses her "wide angle lens" for understanding group phenomena, since she knows that clients act differently when in groups from when they are alone.

Group knowledge includes understanding the impact of such concepts as size, roles, norms, group formation, communication patterns, interpersonal attraction network, mutuality, leadership, homogeneity, cohesion, influence, and group developmental phases. These will be more salient for the work than, say, personal values, individual behavior patterns, or one's possible response to what a participant expresses to others in the group, since these concepts relate to the powerful forces induced by the group context and composition.

Thinking group means considering the group-as-a-whole first, individual participants second when initiating or responding to others. The worker gives up some of her control and shows that she understands there is not merely one, but many helping relationships going on.

By understanding these group phenomena the worker will be more ready to *use* them in all that she does (or refrains from doing) in the group. They will underlie all her own behavior as well as help her make sense of others' behaviors. In effect, these concepts-in-mind precede all else: believing is seeing!

Thinking group is continuously needed whenever more than two persons (you and the client) are present. The worker shows her appreciation of group concepts through the way she engages in the work, through what she sees as important or extraneous or to be expected because of the group situation.

It is hard to illustrate the skill of thinking group since this is an internal mental process, observable or absent as a core basis for interventions. The best we can do here is to cite a worker's description of her work with a group and assume that her belief system is revealed by the importance placed on the particular highlighted concepts. We shall attempt to illustrate differences in frames of reference through some practice excerpts from the literature.

In the first instance, the social worker has an individual orientation. The group experience is open-ended, with seven adult women survivors of incest who met at a family service agency. The screening,

selection, and development throughout what seemed to be a year's
time were carefully described. Let us consider some of the discussion
of this work:

> The primary transference that members enact with a female
> therapist is maternal. Some see her as self-centered and neglectful;
> others view her as a competitor for control of the group; others
> constantly fear overwhelming her with their needs. At some points,
> she is experienced as though she were the abuser. For example,
> during one group meeting I mistakenly revealed what one client
> had felt to be a confidence. She felt I had violated and humiliated
> her before the others, thus taking away her power to decide how
> much to share with them. She doubted she could trust me any
> longer. During subsequent individual and group sessions, the injury
> was worked through, and the transference interpreted.
>
> Any therapeutic error or perceived hurt becomes an opportunity
> to work on trust issues in the transference. Validating the client's
> feelings and taking responsibility for one's mistakes or oversights
> provide an essential corrective experience. "I can see how you felt I
> violated your trust. You must be very angry." . . . At one point in the
> life of the group, I became aware of having fallen into this counter-
> transference trap, encouraging members to express only the nega-
> tive side of their ambivalence toward their abusers. As soon as I was
> ready to hear the other side, they began to speak about their positive
> feelings, as if they had read my mind.[2]

In the brief excerpt above we see the worker's energy focused on
internal dynamics and on the relationship between herself and one
molested adult.

As a contrast, in the following excerpt the worker has a different
focus, the group. The work, also at a family agency, is with an open-
ended group of women in abusive relationships. Emphasis is on the
group itself as the primary helping agent:

> The goals for work with women in abusive relationships became
> fostering autonomy, a sense of empowerment and responsibility, a
> mastery over the environment, and improved self-image. . . . Hope
> and trust are experienced as (their long-kept secret) is shared, not
> with a therapist but with a group of persons who have had the same

experience and are successfully dealing with their problems. . . .
Members participate in many ways: by listening, observing, talking
about their own problems, or relating to and helping others. Though
this experience is intense, the women can choose how they use the
group. Permission to have this choice is empowering. . . .

The members first observe others who are further along in the
learning process. They can identify with that person for hope and
information. Over time, they become the more experienced members who affirm and teach new members. During this process the
group provides a constant reality check. The women's denial and
skewed perceptions about what behavior is abusive are quickly chal-
lenged by other group members. Likewise, as members interact in
the group, they modify misinformation that may have arisen out of
socialization deficits and/or isolation regarding roles, child rearing
techniques, expression of feelings, and personal rights. Many of the
members have never perceived females as powerful or competent.

I serve as a second role model (in addition to their indigenous
leader). . . . I display alternatives to the members' own patterns by
being powerful without being abusive, tender without being abused,
assertive without being aggressive, appreciative of men without being
dependent, autonomous without being isolated, and surely how to
be imperfect without losing self-esteem.[3]

The contrast in emphasis in these two groups is obvious. The
excerpts are all the more interesting since both are from open-ended
groups with abused young women whose needs include decreasing a
sense of isolation and difference, developing self-esteem, and reframing their life view.

Scanning

Scanning involves taking in the whole group with one's eyes. The
worker scans to let her contact be with all the group participants
rather than getting locked into eye-contact with only one or two
people. This is the group version of the "attending" skill (chapter 3)
and is used with a comparable purpose. That is, the social worker
actively takes in diverse communication cues from the other(s) and

conveys her concern for all. Scanning involves sensory, cognitive, and interpersonal communication skills as the worker selectively notices what all the group participants are expressing, in words and in nonverbal ways, and shows that she is connecting with everyone.

In order to scan, the worker shifts her gaze about the group, lingering on no particular person, but not moving so fast or mechanically that she calls attention to a stiffness or routinization in her movements. The scanning should seem natural and expansive, with nonverbal gaze and attentiveness that signal, "I am interested in all of you." By scanning, the social worker helps the group participants feel she is there for all, even when one person may be dominating the communication.

Scanning should occur continuously any time there are more than two persons in the situation. Often group experiences happen in circle formations since this is the fairest way for all to have equal eye contact and communication access to each other and to the worker. However, scanning within a circle requires some special precaution for giving equal notice to the people sitting on each side next to the worker. In fact, careful self-observation of scanning behavior will reveal that one has a particular side (left or right) that is the dominant side. One tends to ignore the person on the other side *unless she deliberately works to balance her gaze equally toward both sides.*

The following episode concerns a group for alcoholics at a Veterans Administration outpatient clinic. It is an open-ended group which meets weekly and is in its second year:

> The men had made a circle and were waiting for me when I came into the room. I looked around at all and said I was glad they had arranged the chairs. There were some nods, Bill and Joe smiled at each other, and I glanced at them with a smile because I figured they had made the arrangement. After a few moments of beginning comments, Gary began to talk about his brother and the problems he was having without a job. He was off on a long tale which did not seem related to what the others expected to talk about. I stopped looking at him, glanced about at the others to see where they were, and also to encourage Gary to cut his story short. Gary took the hint and wound up his tale. I then scanned the group and asked, "What's been happening this week?"

Scanning involves much more than simply looking and listening. It involves seeing and hearing, the outcomes of looking and listening. One can look without seeing and one can listen without hearing!

Fostering Cohesiveness

Groups of people who meet together over time, with or without a worker, either will become increasingly cohesive, or possibly fall apart. Cohesiveness involves an emotional component derived from the interaction of the participants. It is the glue that makes them want to stick together. Ordinarily, the social worker who knows and uses group skills can accelerate this natural process.

Cohesiveness refers to the forces acting on the participants to remain in the group.[4] It can be thought of as high morale, *esprit de corps,* or pride in being in the group. It is seen as commitment to the group and what it does, and is reflected in consistency of attendance, satisfaction in being together, and pressure on the participants to conform to the ways of the group. Regardless of group-type or group purpose, the dynamics of perceived similarity (in-the-same-boat mentality) and shared universality of experience are powerful forces that make group experience helpful to individuals. The social worker fosters cohesiveness in order to promote this mutuality, a common stake in the group's purpose and achievements. She encourages cohesion at all times when with the group or when dealing with group members about group matters aside from meetings.

Cohesiveness is fostered by the words one uses. When talking with or about the group, the worker mainly uses "we," "our," and "us," more than "I," "you," or "yours." This change in vocabulary may seem strange at first, but it very quickly becomes habit and seems natural. Through this simple semantic shift, the worker will convey her feeling about the oneness of the group enterprise rather than a "you" and "them" affair. This says a lot about the worker's positioning of herself within the group and its process.

Here is what it can look like:

Ten people in the Anger and Stress Group came to the Community Center this evening. It was just about time to end the session.

The time went fast with several role plays where they practiced experiencing angry impulses and visualizing an alternative response to their accustomed behavior. I said, "We did some hard things tonight." Jean and Tom nodded. The others just looked at me and seemed to sigh. I continued, "We are finding it easier each week to discover new ways to handle stressful situations."

8. Skills for Building Groups

> In a shared activity, each person refers what he (or she) is doing
> to what the other is doing and *vice-versa*. That is, the activity of
> each is placed in the same inclusive situation. To pull at a rope at
> which others happen to be pulling is not a shared or conjoint
> activity, unless the pulling is done with knowledge that others are
> pulling and for the sake of either helping or hindering what they
> are doing.
>
> John Dewey

In this chapter we shall discuss five skills which we have identified as
especially important for building the group. These are selecting communication patterns purposely, voicing group achievements, preserving group history and continuity, verbalizing norms, and encouraging
development of traditions and rituals.

We consider these skills and those which we shall identify in
chapter 10 to be *contingent* group skills. That is, they are not opera-
tive continuously, as are those in chapter 7 (thinking group, scanning,
fostering cohesion). They are used in certain circumstances according
to the dictates of the situation. As such, these context-based skills are
used when the impinging group process signals to the worker that
group building actions are in order. This chapter describes each skill,
discusses when it should be used, and illustrates its use.

These skills are geared to foster the group aspect of the group, or
its groupness. Skills for groupness are used contingent upon particular sets of circumstances, while the key continuous group skills (see
chapter 7) are used all the time.

Groupness refers to the essential quality of a group that distin-
guishes it from being merely an aggregate of individuals or a collectivity.[1] Workers who appreciate groupness see the group members as co-
partners in the group enterprise, share their control, and increasingly
give away their power to the participants (empower them); and use

group level interventions rather than intrapersonal level ones to accomplish these aims.

Groupness is valued variably by workers depending on their knowledge of particular skills for enhancing it, on how they view themselves and their role, and on the purpose of the group.[2] While groups are increasingly popular, they are often led by workers who never took a class in group theory or practice and who pursue their own special purposes with the groupness component being merely incidental. Learning the how-to's of group work is often done by trial and error, by watching others, by sink-or-swim-but-do-it mentalities, or not at all. Many brave persons have become mini-group-gurus through such routes. However, without familiarity with group theory, dynamics, and other particulars, it is hard to imagine workers intentionally affecting the groupness in a positive way. Some may do this guided by their intuition. We aim to highlight some particulars for deliberately achieving groupness in this chapter.

Groupness exists on a continuum. If the worker views herself as a specialist who is there to do certain things *to* the group members (e.g., educate, rehabilitate), then there probably will be less groupness cultivated. If the worker is there to facilitate the group's purpose, on the other hand, there is more room for attention to groupness but also room for domination by one group participant or for a clique within the group to take over the direction of the group. In such instances, groupness is a happy accident. But the worker who sees her role as mediating the transactions among the participants, as attending to the group process so that participants can take increasing responsibility for their group life, will be focused on the group as a whole and intentionally focused on enhancing the groupness of the group. It is to some skills for enhancing groupness that we now turn.

Selecting Communication Patterns Purposefully

The worker does much to set the tone of the group meeting by encouraging a communication pattern that balances the "air-time" available to all the participants. Unlike the nonverbal ways of communicating feelings and messages (e.g., frowns, hand gestures) or the doing-oriented activities where many can be involved at the same

time (e.g., eating, dancing), when it comes to talking there can*not* be
a Tower of Babel. Most group participants develop courteous turn-
talking patterns for their discussions which reflect a valuation of
fairness; e.g., only one person should talk at a time, but not too long;
the quiet ones ought to get the chance to have their say.

But groups are also subject to the vagaries of needy individuals, to
spirited controversies with politeness thrown to the winds, and to the
influence of alienated or passive participants. They are also influenced
by the prescriptions of culturally embedded norms that may foster
skewed participation, e.g., adults may be more vocal than teenagers,
males may be more dominant than females, majority supporters may
be intolerant of others' views, ethnic/racial minorities in small numbers in the group may be discounted. Meetings often can get out of
hand, a signal to the group-conscious worker to help the group regain
its equilibrium.

The social worker helps the group become aware of the need for
"verbal traffic-management" through helping it purposely establish its
pattern of communication and develop ways for sticking on course.
This is no easy matter. Even with good intentions groups often get
out of hand. We have identified certain skills in chapter 11 as useful
for engaging barriers; and they, like all the skills identified as useful
in work with individuals, are appropriate in certain group situations.
And we shall deal further with such difficulties in chapter 10 when
we discuss the skill, inviting full participation, a way of working
within any given pattern of communication in order to facilitate the
work of the group. Selecting communication patterns purposefully,
our focus in this chapter, is used prior to inviting full participation
and, in fact, often precludes the need for it.

To select a communication pattern purposefully is to make a judgment about an assumed facilitative communication format that is
consistent with the group's purpose, size, and stage of development,
and to set it in motion. This may happen at the start of a group's
experience, at the beginning of any session, or at any time during the
session if a change of pace or direction seems indicated and the group
participants reveal their willingness to go along with the proposed
format. Several communication patterns are possible for a given group
and these may fluctuate in different sessions or even within any one
session.

The Maypole: the worker, teacher, or group leader talks to individuals one-by-one. Individuals direct responses to the central person. There is little between-member communication. The worker dominates and controls.

In the meeting below with a group of men who were violent and abusive in their relationship with women, the worker initiates the session with a *maypole* format. This is a frequent pattern in groups where information giving is the priority. It is well known as the predominant way that lecture-discussion groups are conducted.

I opened the session with a description of violence: its causes, why it is a problem, and why it should be stopped. I asked, "Has any one found a way to control anger when it mounts up?" Mr. Ashley said he tried to count to ten and sometimes that works. "Who else has a method?" Mr. Downs commented that any method he tries escapes him during arguments. I said, "It *is* hard to do. Any other ideas? . . ."

The Round Robin: each participant speaks in turn (usually clockwise) in relation to a given focus set by the worker. The worker is still in control (more subtly), often nonverbally signaling the progression via eye contact and head-nod.

The worker initiates a *round robin* pattern in the following illustration, opening this session of a meeting with abusing mothers. "How did you get along this week? Let's start, with Joan." Joan says, "I only lost my temper once with Jeremy. I was furious with how he had messed up his room again right after I had cleaned it up. But I did not hit him; I just yelled." "OK. Good. Next." The worker nods her head and stares at Kim seated next to Joan.

Another example drawn from the fifth meeting of the men who were violent and abusive in their relationships: the worker says, "I'd like to start this day with our thinking about this question: what qualities or characteristics do you value in your relationship with your partner? Let's go around the circle and each man speak to this point. . . . Mr. Lambert . . ."

The Hot Seat: the worker (and group) engage in an extended back and forth discussion with one participant. The others are mainly a watchful and sometimes participating audience. This may be thought of as an extended-over-time *round robin.* For example, John presents his situation this week for half the session and June for the second half. In each session a comparable A/B format prevails with the next presenting persons designated at the conclusion of a session. Or, the plan may involve only one presenting situation each week. In any case the underlying structure for the meetings is known by all and this orders the sequences.

The following episode concerns a staff meeting in a residence for pregnant unmarried women. The supervisor opens the discussion. "Now we can turn to our 'Clinic Time' for the last hour of our meeting today. Last week we focused on Jeanine's problems with helping Muriel stay in school. I think we should first have an update from Jeanine on what has happened this week and which if any of our ideas were helpful. Then it is Marilyn's turn. Marilyn has asked to present her work with Susan to see if we can come up with a different way to involve Susan's parents to be more supportive of her. OK Jeanine . . ."

The Agenda-Controlled: in task groups and more formal associations the minutes, old business, new business, and so forth form the structure and sequence of the communication pattern. Other Robert's Rules structure who, how, when, and to whom participants may speak.

We shall not present an *agenda-controlled* situation. We believe this is a too familiar pattern that needs no illustration.

The Free Form: group participants take responsibility to speak with any other person according to what is being said and who is contributing or silent. In this pattern a large degree of responsibility for the flow and form of the discussion rests with the participants as they learn, with the worker's help, matters of turn-taking, consideration, risking, confronting, and so forth. The *free-form* pattern can emerge when the participants become familiar with each other and the worker encourages their responsibility for the group process.

We enter the fifth session of a group for battering husbands.

> Some men related incidents of violence that were not related to their
> wives. One member talked about wanting to shoot a neighbor's dog
> who would not stop barking. Another member talked about a work-
> related incident when he lost his temper. The members continued
> to refuse to take responsibility for their violent acts and to blame
> them on sources beyond their control. I said, "I see you are so busy
> putting the blame for your violence outside you that we are getting
> off the point of how you can work at controlling your violent im-
> pulses." A moment of silence. Mr. Lamb looked at Mr. King and
> said, "How have you gotten along with the plans you told us about
> last week?" Mr. King then launched forth with a description of his
> experiences. Mr. Corning perked up and commented.

Voicing Group Achievements

To voice group achievements is to verbally summarize with appreciation any indications of progress or growth the worker has noticed as
exhibited by the group or particular individuals. These may be actions
or thoughts or feelings that may or may not have been noticed by the
others. The worker periodically calls attention to benchmark movement and especially in the aftermath of reviewing some outstanding
experience or event. The worker may recall achievements and progress retrospectively, when the group is considering new directions or
projects, when visitors or new participants are present, when the
group seems to flounder, dissipate its energies, appear disinterested
in its work, or approach its conclusion. The worker may also plan to
voice group achievements as a routine in helping the group assess
itself.

In the instance below, the social worker was meeting with a group
of adults molested as children and the session opened with very little
energy being expressed by anyone:

> It seemed hard to get off the ground at the start of this session. I
> said, "I was particularly impressed with how hard we worked last
> week. We risked talking about some painful memories, and al-

though this was hard to do, I think it was gutsy and in the long run this will be helpful." Jenny said it was hard and she had to work at coming back this week. There was an audible sigh from many of the others. Dorothy looked around and said she has been coming here for more than a year now and it gets easier each time.

Preserving Group History and Continuity

The illustration just cited does more than just show the worker voicing group achievements. It also shows the worker preserving the group's continuity. The worker can preserve group history and continuity by reminding the group of previous experiences in the group (both positive and negative ones), by deliberately linking the current session to the previous one by referring to what happened last week in a summarizing sentence, or helping the group develop symbols of their past experiences. The worker provides continuity at the start of a session, refers to past history periodically when the group appears to be in a reflective mood, when the group seems stymied, when the group is in a planning or assessment phase, and always as part of the ending phase of a group's experience.

The episode in this group of recovering alcoholics shows the participants using a linking structure which preserves continuity.

> The group began, as usual, with reactions to last week. I asked them if they had any more thoughts about last week or any that had occurred to them during the week. The group members shared and ventilated feelings about the previous session. However, reactions were minimal and took only about five minutes. They were appreciative of the risks taken by one relatively new participant the week before. Susan stated that she had enjoyed getting to know Margaret. Later in this session, they were thinking about limiting each person's talk-time to three minutes. I reminded them that we had tried this two month's ago and only succeeded in generating many hard feelings. Did they want to try this again?

In a group of older adults that had been meeting for two years at a day treatment center, a new woman entered.

Miss Gans appeared and was ushered to a seat by the president, Mrs. Lowry. At Mrs. Lowry's urging, the other men and women gave their names and welcomed Miss Gans. Then Mrs. Lowry brought out the group scrapbook and showed her pictures of the group's various picnics and outings. The first pages had snapshots of each member, their signature, address and telephone number. <u>I asked Mr. Burns if he wanted to take a picture of Miss Gans.</u> He smiled his assent, went to the closet, and appeared with the group's Poloroid camera. Then he asked Miss Gans to stand so that he could take her picture and add it to their scrapbook. Miss Gans smiled timidly and went to one side of the room with him.

An example of a group's preserving their history as they faced their ending and separation is presented in the classic account of stages of group development by Garland, Jones, and Kolodny as "review . . . a conscious process of reminiscing about club life and events":

> [They reminisced] with me about the things they did together, the fun they had, some of the hard times, some of the trouble that members had gotten into, places they had been, and how much bigger they are now compared to when the club began. [Then they] shifted into the area of behavior, with some saying that they don't do some of the things they used to, like stealing, breaking into the Neighborhood House, having the cops chase them.[3]

Verbalizing Norms

All groups have norms which provide boundaries, limits, and focus to their activities and enable them to conduct their "business" in a fairly orderly manner. Norms are rules for the behavior of participants in a particular group. Norms, also known as ground rules, stipulate how to be and not be, what it is OK to do and not OK to do.

Some rules derive from the agency sponsorship, e.g., only veterans may belong; meetings must end by ten o'clock; meetings last only one-and-a-half hours; a certain fee is paid each week. Norms derive from generally accepted culture-based rules of conduct, e.g., don't pick on a person when they're down; respect your seniors; no profanity in mixed gender groups. Still others are formulated out of a particular group's experience and determination, and these norms are the thumb print of a given group. That is, they make for the uniqueness of the particular group, differentiating it from other groups. Or they distinguish this group as being part of a larger organization of similar purpose groups. For example, members of Alcoholics Anonymous groups will use first names only; members of Recovery, Inc. will use Recovery Language—"endorsement," "nervous symptoms," "self-spotting," etc., and follow Recovery rules such as "try to be average; will to bear discomfort."[4]

Other norms (group rules of conduct) pertain to such things as confidentiality, having or not having guests, attendance responsibility, care of furniture and other equipment, smoking, eating, dress code, and so forth. As is the case with special traditions (which will be discussed subsequently), the self-help group, in particular, is governed by norms that control the behavior of members and spell its uniqueness. Group norms create an in-group, a community of informed participants, which to a great extent accentuates the groupness aspect of the group, creating a we/they mentality and enhancing group bond.

Here are the ground rules of the Toronto Addicted Women's Self-Help Group:

- the entire group is involved in decision-making

- the membership is open and ongoing

- the group decides to welcome (or not to) new members

- meetings are open: women can bring friends

- women agree to confidentiality; i.e., information shared does not go beyond the group

- women agree not to share drugs

- women agree not to "self-trash," i.e., not to put themselves down in the group[5]

Some norms are verbalized, perhaps as part of each meeting, and are a conscious piece of every session; e.g., a girl scout's honor is to be trusted. Other norms are unspoken and covert. They are picked up through modeling others' behavior and being socialized into the ways of the group through participating in its life.

Some covert norms are deleterious to group growth and to member welfare. For example, a group may allow members to verbally attack others. That is, members will not intervene to support another member who is being attacked or to stop the attacking member. In such an instance, the worker can verbalize the pattern that seems to be allowed and ask the group if they purposely want to keep this previously unspoken norm or if they would like to change it.

The social worker verbalizes norms as one means for calling attention to the groupness of the group. The worker asks the group members to recall a norm or mentions the avowed norm herself openly from time to time as a means of reinforcing rules the group has made. The worker points to group norms when certain rules seem to be forgotten or ignored, when new members need to have some background on how the group functions or an explanation for particular actions.

In the following example, we see a piece of a Halloween Party for boys, six to nine years of age, in a group residence for emotionally disturbed foster children:

> The boys got dressed in their costumes and I helped them. Ronnie quickly put on his Frankenstein costume and proceeded to act scary and monstrous. Mel used a nightcap, a nightshirt, a white stick, and a tube of red lipstick to turn himself into a very convincing case of measles. Some of the other boys accused him of using this as an excuse to suck his thumb and carry a stuffed animal. I reminded them that we had decided not to tease each other at this party.

In this brief episode, we see the worker pointing out a group determined norm instead of arbitrarily disapproving of a behavior. A group empowering intervention is a far more effective one.

Encouraging Development of Traditions and Rituals

Closely related to group norms are special traditions and rituals which groups evolve over time or which they adopt when affiliating with a parent national organization. These elements heighten group identity and develop a spirit of loyalty to the group as the members strive to conform to behavior expected of members of the parent group. Often the traditions and rituals, which are aspects of group structure, are the ideology which binds the group members together and exerts a commanding, directional force on the participants. In the case of self-help groups, this ideology and its trappings serve an executive function. That is, the ideology guides the behavior of the group in such a way that, for example, the group can function with rotating leaders, with no one central leadership person. These elements are the stuff of self-help.

To encourage development of traditions and rituals the social worker understands these symbols of group identity, supports opportunities for their expression, and suggests the creation of such trappings where none exist. Rituals may be developed to start or end meetings, to be part of special events, to signal the termination of a series of meetings, and to connect with other groups or entities in the wider community. Symbols or symbolic behavior may exist as an expected part of meetings or also serve to remind members of the group at other times when they are not involved in a session.

For example, the structure of a buddy or "special person" system in which group members exchange telephone numbers and are directed to call one another between meetings or in a crisis situation extends the helpfulness of the group from weekly or monthly meetings to an everyday affair. AA groups are a prototype for many other self-help groups, especially valuable in the area of addiction. The Serenity Prayer may be used either to start or end the meeting, and is an example of a powerful ritual:

> God grant me the strength to accept the things I cannot change, the courage to change things I can, and the wisdom to know the difference.

The twelve steps are also forceful in helping the members keep on track. Consider step one, a step which members must return to repeatedly whenever they falter: "Anonymity is the spiritual foundation of all our traditions ever reminding us to place principles before personalities." Other rituals, symbols, and structures used to enhance loyalty to the tenets of the group and its purpose include telling one's story, observing "birthdays," and using chips or reward tokens.

Another example of symbols that elicit pride and hold a group together can be seen in the Night Hawks, a cadre of high school boys who patrol the housing projects as a way of preventing crime and keeping order. They have outfits like the Green Berets and radios which serve to set them off from others, according them prestige and respect.

Some groups end with a special circle hand clasp through which they "pass the spark of friendship" or a group hug or other symbolic gesture. In some AMAC groups (adults molested as children) it is a tradition to join hands and proclaim, "It is not my fault. I am not to blame."

In cases such as these and the many other variants which workers may find groups employing, the main behavior for the worker is to support these symbols and actions, and encourage the group in its we-ness. We turn now in chapter 9 to consider skills for facilitating the work of the group.

9. Skills for Facilitating the Work of the Group

> Whatever it is that generates the human want for social contact and for companionship, the effect seems to take two forms: a need for an audience before which to try out one's vaunted selves, and a need for teammates with whom to enter into collusive intimacies and backstage relaxation.
>
> Erving Goffman

In working with groups, the social worker faces all the same challenges that confront her when she works with individuals, and more; for her work still involves dealing accurately with communication exchanges, and with the obvious and subtle meanings they contain. Therefore, the skills required in working with individuals, especially those for "dealing with feelings" and "dealing with information," described in chapters 4 and 5, continue to be important. With the addition of people to the worker-client situation, additional complexities and opportunities are introduced, so that additional, special skills are also required, skills particularly suited to dealing with more than one other person at a time. Some of these skills are described and illustrated in this chapter.

"Skills for facilitating the work of the group" are addressed to helping the participants help each other, helping them to deal with issues and problems, express what they really mean, stay focused on the work at hand, and be open to all in the discussions. They should be thought of as skills concerned with *process* more than *outcome*. That is, the social worker tries to help the group participants pursue their purpose in as open and fair a manner as possible, with consideration for the needs and interests of everyone.

Skills for facilitating the work of the group include amplifying subtle messages, softening overpowering messages, reaching for a feeling link, reaching for an information link, redirecting messages, inviting full participation, turning issues back to the group, reaching for consensus, and reaching for difference.

Amplifying Subtle Messages

To amplify a subtle message is to call attention to unnoticed communicative behavior—words, tone of voice, facial expressions—by verbalizing it. The worker amplifies a subtle message when these three conditions occur: more than two persons are present; one person's behavior is incongruous with the situation (e.g., everyone is laughing but one person is silent and stares at the floor); and others present do not seem to notice the behavior. The idea is to call attention to the fact that a message has been sent. Therefore, the worker should direct her comment to the others, not to the person whose behavior she is commenting on.

It should be noted that nonverbal behaviors are not, in and of themselves, subtle. Sometimes others present *do* notice one person's frown or clenched fist. Sometimes they respond to it and sometimes they choose not to respond. In either event, the social worker should not amplify, for the others do notice. In the second instance, however, it is appropriate for the worker to reach for the person's feelings.

When other persons are not present, the social worker has no need to amplify a subtle message, because there is no one present who has not noticed. In this instance it is also appropriate for the worker to reach for feelings. It is an instance of work with individuals, and skills for work with individuals apply.

Subtle messages that sometimes require amplification in a group situation inhere in such aspects of behavior as rapidity of speech, loudness, pitch, speech errors or pauses, timing, and sarcasm (a special instance where inconsistent combinations of verbal and nonverbal cues convey feelings in a faint way). Subtle messages may also be communicated through posture, gesture, facial expression, or eye movements.[1] Implicit in the skill of amplifying subtle messages is worker recognition that, when more than one person is involved in a discussion, it is difficult and often awkward for the persons involved to take turns and speak in an orderly sequence. Frequently, several persons would like to express themselves at once; sometimes the loudest or more persistent one is successful in monopolizing the discussion while the others are forced to live with their own reactions, but not express them verbally.

Messages are sometimes sent through subtle ways because it is hard to stand against others and differ with a dominant opinion, because it is hard to express feelings, and because some individuals are not so vocal as others. Many subtle messages are missed by the parties in their eagerness to have their say. And many are missed by the social worker, too, because it is difficult to attend to several persons' cues at the same time. Nonetheless, the worker needs to be alert to as many subtle cues as possible, and amplify them when appropriate. She must busily scan the cues sent simultaneously by all parties to the interaction, in order to point out discrepancies as she sees and hears them, so that these messages and their senders may gain an audience.

In all communication, messages are continuously being sent at two levels: the literal, content level; and the metacommunication level (messages about how the specific content should be taken).[2] Metacommunication messages, often conveyed through subtle means, may signal attitudes about the message; e.g., take this seriously, or I'm really kidding; attitudes about one's self, e.g., I am bored, or I feel ignored; or attitudes about the others, e.g., they don't care about me, or they irritate me. By attending to both communication levels, the worker is attending to two aspects of the message: what the actual statement is, and what is being asked of the other (e.g., agree with me; don't believe what I am saying). And by noticing the expressive behavior of those persons other than the ones who might be holding forth verbally at a given time, she expands the possibilities for others to join the exchange.

In the following example, the social worker amplifies Mr. Hart's messages (head shaking and muttering) which were subtle and unnoticed by the others.

I made a home visit to see Mr. Hart, a blind, sixty-eight-year-old veteran, who lives with his daughter and son-in-law. The three of them met with me in the living room. All were speaking at the same time, trying to get my attention. Mr. Hart was the least successful and began shaking his head and muttering. I said, "Mr. Hart's shaking his head." The other two stopped and looked at him.

In the next example, the worker uses this behavior in a group situation when he notices Miss Royal's foot and hand movements.

Mr. Carson was talking to the group and lecturing that they shouldn't expect the worker to push them along. They should cooperate and not act like ostriches, putting their heads in the ground. I noticed Miss Royal, who was sitting next to me shuffling her feet and twisting her handkerchief for some minutes. I said to the group, "Miss Royal looks like she has something to say." All eyes turned to her. Miss Royal then said that she agreed with Mr. Carson's point, smiled, and pulled her chair closer to the table.

The following illustration again shows the social worker noticing subtle cues (closed eyes and slight smile) and calling the group's attention to them.

During one segment of the employee committee meeting, grievances to be presented to the agency administrator were being discussed. All grievances were being given cursory examination and added to the list. Mrs. Cain was sitting opposite me with her eyes closed and a slight smile on her lips. I said, "Mrs. Cain is sitting here smiling." Miss Joyce said, "What are you thinking, Louise?" Mrs. Cain hesitated a moment and then said, "This is ridiculous; if we present all these grievances at once, no one will listen to us." Other members supported her position and a discussion of her motion ensued.

In the next two examples group members are struggling to express feelings. Unpleasant feelings are particularly hard to volunteer. In the first instance, the worker points out an uncomfortable look, while in the second instance a frown is the key to interrupting the process to amplify one person's subtle message.

At a meeting in the lounge of the housing project to discuss specific instances of inadequate security, I notice Mrs. O'Neil sitting by herself and looking uncomfortable. She was wringing her hands. I said that Mrs. O'Neil looked uncomfortable. A couple of people asked her what was wrong, and she said that she came to the meeting because Mrs. Miller asked her to, but that she's seventy-five years old and she doesn't want the manager to think she's a troublemaker.

Later in the meeting, Mr. Downs and the group needed a rule about how long anyone could talk. He said that nobody should talk for more than a minute because some of them would get started about their aches and pains and use up all the time. Someone else said they shouldn't talk about sickness. A few people agreed. Mr. Goins was frowning during the entire interaction. I said, "Mr. Goins is frowning." Several group members turned to him and someone asked what was the matter. He said that sickness was one of the big problems when you're old and it should be talked about here. He said that if they couldn't talk about it to each other, who could they talk to about it? There was lots of agreement.

Softening Overpowering Messages

To soften an overpowering message is to verbalize the essence of a highly affective message (shouts, punches, glares) so that the strength of the affect is reduced and the message can be "heard." Overpowering messages should be softened when there is indication that the others cannot deal with the message at the intensity or pitch at which they are expressed.

Using this skill does not mean softening loud talking or actions if the persons involved are used to expressing themselves in such ways. For workers are not concerned here with decorum, politeness, or "adult ways of expressing anger." Boys often express all kinds of feeling physically and *can handle this*. Likewise, family members often shout at each other and are quite able to bear each other's anger. Nor is concern for the worker's personal comfort—quiet or orderliness —justification for the act.

The worker moves in to the interaction and asks by words or actions that the message be softened when more than two persons are present, and she notices the others cannot deal with it in its present form. By reducing the affect, the worker makes it possible for the person to "hear" the content of the message, content that otherwise would be obliterated by the powerful affect.

In the following example, the social worker in a meeting of pre-school mothers softens the message by commenting on the group's anger with one person.

> While Mrs. Allen was opening the meeting with a prayer, Mrs. Sellers began to laugh. Mrs. Allen stopped her prayer and, along with the other group members, turned her attention to the laughing Mrs. Sellers. The faces of the group members became rigid with a collective look of anger as they silently focused their eyes on Mrs. Sellers who had stopped laughing. The silence lasted about fifteen seconds. Then Mrs. Allen, looking straight at Mrs. Sellers, said, "If you laugh once more when God's words are spoken in this group, you will no longer be a member of this group." Still looking at Mrs. Sellers, the others in the group nodded in approval. I said, "Mrs. Sellers the group is pretty angry at you."

It should be noted that this skill requires that the worker repeat what the group is expressing, using words rather than affect. If she had directed her comments to elicit a response from Mrs. Sellers at that moment ("Mrs. Sellers, you look upset at what the group members said"), this would *not* be softening an overpowering message. Rather, the worker would be reaching for feelings.

Reaching for a Feeling Link

To reach for a feeling link is to ask others to connect with a feeling being expressed. This skill is appropriate to use when more than two persons are present, and a feeling is expressed. In situations where a feeling is expressed but the worker is meeting with only one other person, the proper skill to use is getting with feelings.

In situations that meet both conditions, however, the worker is not the only person who can demonstrate to another that one's inner experience has been understood. Every person present at the time a feeling is expressed has the potential to empathize and to communicate that empathy, and the social worker reaches for a feeling link in order to realize that potential. That is, when others are present, she is not the only helper and should not act this way by getting with feelings. Rather, she should reach for a feeling link.

In the first example, the worker reaches for a feeling between a troubled junior high school boy and some of his classmates.

Dan asked the other boys if anyone could crash him that night (let him sleep at their house). Timothy said, "A-gain, man?" Dan flashed his eyes at Timothy, then retreated to a corner and stared at the floor. I said that Dan looked pretty upset. Timothy said he couldn't help that, that his mother told him if he brought Dan home one more time this week she'd throw them both out in the street. Rob asked Dan what was the matter with his own house. Dan didn't answer. Timothy played with his shoelace and mumbled that Dan can't go home when his mother's working. Dan shouted at Tim that Tim better shut up or he'd waste him. There was some silence during which a few of the boys glanced at Dan, and Tim kept playing with his shoelace. I asked if anyone could imagine what Dan must be feeling. Tim nodded. Ernie said that Dan must be mad. Tim said, "And embarrassed." Dan looked over at the group, then sat down where he was. Rob asked Dan if he wanted to go home with him. Dan moved a little closer to the group and asked Rob if he had to ask his mother. "She don't care," Rob answered, and moved closer to Dan. Ernie said if Dan wanted, he could stay with him next time. Tim said that by next week Dan could probably stay with him a couple of night again, too.

The next excerpt occurred at the second session of a Job Search and Survival training program. The worker reaches for a feeling link when one man expresses his uncertainties in a discussion where the others seemed to convey only confidence.

I summarized the various self-presentation skills that we had dealt with today and said these would help them show their best potentials when they applied for their next job. I added that these, while not the easiest to do, have helped others from job search groups in the past. There were several affirmative comments. Mr. Coles said he would practice this assertive behavior and was eager to try it out. Mr. Turner said this has added to his self-confidence and some others nodded assent. That seemed to end the discussion. But then Mr. Jones said in a soft voice that he was still scared about applying for a job again. He added that he had been turned down so many times before. I asked if any one else was feeling some of what Mr. Jones was feeling right now. Mr. Carpenter said he was scared too. Others now expressed how hesitant they really were.

In the following instance, the worker reaches for a feeling link after amplifying a subtle message in dealing with a couple.

An elderly couple came to discuss what they could do with their retarded forty-two year old son when they could no longer care for him. Mrs. Pitt did most of the talking while Mr. Pitt sat silent clenching his fists. I said, "Mr. Pitt is clenching his fists." Mrs. Pitt looked up in surprise and said, "Well he is." I said, "Can you imagine what Mr. Pitt is feeling now?" Mrs. Pitt remained silent for a moment; then she said, "I guess he is feeling scared that he can't take care of Junior. I felt the same way when we brought him home from the hospital."

Finally, we see the worker reaching for a feeling link in a different group situation:

In a monthly support group there were five members present to discuss their concerns of caring for someone with Alzheimer's Disease. Mrs. Hall stated she felt like getting into the car and driving away, never to return. Then she said she knew that she couldn't leave her husband. Silence . . . I said, "Has anyone ever felt a little bit like Mrs. Hall is feeling now?" Mrs. Singer said she felt that way lots of times and two others agreed with her.

Reaching for an Information Link

To reach for an information link is to ask others to connect with a statement or question that someone has expressed. This skill is appropriate to use when more than two persons are present, and others probably have sufficient information to respond to the matter involved.

Often, group participants will direct their communication to the worker and expect some response. They have learned in other experiences that the worker (teacher, therapist, sponsor, or some authority figure) expects to supply special knowledge to deal with the raised comments and that they are not supposed to do so. By reaching for an information link, the worker shows she is not the only "expert" in the situation. The worker gives back her (assumed) power to the others by signaling that *they* are the ones best able to respond to their issues out of their own experiences. Furthermore, the worker implies by this action that she expects that they will help each other.

In the following example the social worker reaches for an information link during a house meeting with teen-age residents of a group home.

> They were complaining about how difficult it was to keep in touch with their friends from home because of all the rules. Jean said telephone time was too short for the number of persons who needed to make calls. Lee talked about the curfew and lights-out rules on week nights. Ellie said it took a while for anyone new to the Home to understand all the things about living here. Lois, the newest resident, turned to me and asked how she could ever figure out what was OK and not OK to do here. I wondered if others could fill her in about the important things. Barbara said she would go over the main rules with Lois. Gloria added that she would show her where the schedules were posted. Amy promised to help her with the sign-up chores. Jean asked that they get back to their telephone complaints.

In this instance the worker could have answered Lois with some comments on how others had learned to get settled into the home. But she reached for an information link instead, knowing that more real help could come from other residents who had experienced the situation themselves.

Redirecting Messages

To redirect a message is to ask an individual whose message is intended for another to direct his statement or feeling to that person, whether that person is present or not. This behavior is used when more than two persons are present and the person directs his message to the worker or other(s) in the situation while the one for whom the message is intended is there hearing it. It is also used when the person gives the worker a message intended for someone who is not present. This may occur with the worker alone or with the worker while others are there too.

An assumption underlying the use of this behavior is that people are able to manage their own affairs even though it is difficult and uncomfortable to do so at times. In much the same way as the social worker gives his attention to helping the client take responsibility for making his direct communication as clear and congruent as possible, so does he show the other how ineffective his expression of fact, opinion, or feeling is if it is directed at the wrong target. Misplaced, behind-the-back messages may bring other satisfactions to the sender (relief from pent-up feelings, revenge through influencing others, sympathy from others), but they do nothing toward clearing the air. Worse, they may generate many half-truths and increase misinformation now possessed by others beyond the parties involved, and they may dissipate the energy from where the real work lies.

By redirecting messages where they are intended, the social worker is also conveying his own metamessage to the others about the kind of help he offers. That is, he will do what he can to open up lines of communication that have become clogged; he will not get into one side of a problem and then become a messenger who carries the information back and forth between the others. Often persons appeal to the worker, the wrong target for the message, to use his sanction as added power against the other person. Such approaches to settling difficulties may have worked in the past ("Mommy, Johnny is picking on me!").[3] If the social worker falls into such a trap, his metamessage to the client is something like, "Yes, I *do* know better than you what you can say and do. Yes, I will take care of you."

In redirecting the message, the social worker must be careful through tone of voice, facial expression, and words to make this move something other than a put-down or turn-off of the other. That is, the worker withholds his involvement *not* because he does not care, but because he cares so much that the client take his difficulty to the proper place where he may get results. It is easier for the social worker to redirect matters of information than feeling issues ("You should be asking Miss Taylor; she is the one who can tell you") because it is obvious that the worker may not have the information, and may not be able to implement the request.

Matters of feeling are much more seductive; for the worker might secretly want to counsel and advise the other in his interpersonal behavior. Or he might use such opportunities to gather more information for his own use at some future time. For example, take an instance in which a group member complains to the worker after the meeting about how ineffective the president was. If the worker becomes involved in exploring this, or influencing the complaining member in any direction, he does so only out of such motives as curiosity about how others think the meeting went, or need to protect (or undermine) the president. To affect the course of future meetings, the worker must direct such a reaction back to the person(s) involved —either the president or, better, the total group.

In the following example, the social worker avoids what might be viewed as a handle to get into a mother's feelings about her mothering by directing her question to a future discussion with her children.

> I was talking with the mother of one of the fifth-grade children. She told me how busy she was because she worked and was also involved in a number of parent groups. She then said, "I wonder if my not being at home more bothers the children." I replied, "Did you ever ask your children how they feel about it?"

In the next example, with a husband and wife, the worker redirects the husband's message and thus avoids placing herself between the two, who must work on their own difficulties.

> Mrs. Jenkins told her husband that he doesn't care about her, that if he did he wouldn't run around with all those other girls. Mr. Jenkins leaned toward me and said in a high-pitched voice that he loved his wife and that the other girls don't mean anything to him. I told him that he should be telling that to Mrs. Jenkins; for she is the one who feels he doesn't care.

The following example shows the worker redirecting a message to open up lines of communication between two persons who had stopped speaking.

I was sitting between Mrs. Root and Mrs. Hicks who had had an argument last week. Mrs. Root said that Mrs. Hicks had really hurt her feelings. <u>I said, "Why don't you tell Mrs. Hicks about it."</u>

The next two illustrations show the worker redirecting a message within a group in such a way that the entire group is affected by the behavior. In both instances the worker is conveying the message, that she will not do the group's work. She redirects their message to her back to them.

The older adult group was making final preparations for their trip when Rita leaned over and whispered to me that I'd better remind Agatha to pay. <u>I told her that she could remind Agatha, that she didn't need me to do it for her.</u> Then, when there was a pause in the group discussion, Rita said, "Everybody paid for the trip but Agatha." Agatha said, "Oh! I almost forgot again!," as she began rifling through her purse. "Here; it's already in an envelope," she continued, extending her arm forward to show that it was. "Pass it around to Rita," she said, handing it to the woman on her right.

In one of her group sessions we were discussing an issue current at the school. All the interaction was directed at me even though there were two very strong opposing factions who could have been directing their comments to one another. This session occurred right after the black students had presented their Black History Week program. The white students were telling me that they were upset by the content of the program while the black students were telling me that the program was not meant to offend white students. Since all these comments were aimed at me, <u>I suggested that the comments be directed toward one another rather than toward me.</u>

Before moving on to consider other skills for facilitating the work of the group, it should be noted that the skills presented up to this point deal mainly with feelings. That is, amplifying and softening messages, reaching for feeling links, and redirecting messages are especially geared to clarifying and attending to the affective part of communications. There is also a frequently occurring pattern in the sequencing of these skills which is illustrated in the next excerpt of a group meeting. The sequence seems to be amplify or soften a message, then redirect the message. In the episode below, a small group of people with AIDS are meeting with their social worker. Four persons are returning group members who have been together for more than a year. One new member, Bob, entered in this session.

Terry said, "I just feel like sometimes it isn't worth it. It's so damn useless. I mean, we have to fight for everything we have. First it was fighting to keep my job. Then I was so sick even I knew I couldn't work. Then I had to fight for my disability. I am so tired of fighting. Now I'm fighting my lousy blood count." (His hands are over his face, tearful). I said, "Has anyone felt like Terry is feeling right now?" (Reaching for a feeling link.) Arnie replied, "Yeh, for me it comes and goes. Some days I wonder if it is all worth the fight. Some days I want to die. I hate this disease, but . . . I like being alive. As lousy as I feel sometimes, I still want to live. I am afraid of not fighting." Silence. The worker noticed John smiling but none of the group noticing. I said, "John is smiling." (Amplifying a subtle message.) Arnie asked, "What is so funny?" John replied, "Not funny . . . it's faith. I really believe that we can beat this monster. I can remember those days you are describing. I used to just stay in bed. One day I decided that I would beat this monster by overdosing. I didn't die. Only God knows why. From that day on I decided that it was the damn depression that was killing me." Turning to the worker John said, "Tell this new guy we can make it." I said, "John, you tell Bob." (Redirecting a message.) John then said, "You can make it, man. You look scared to death. It doesn't have to be that way. I was diagnosed three, nearly four years ago. Don't let the monster get you down. It's depression that will kill you if you let it."

As the worker reflected silently after this episode, it is of utmost importance for persons with AIDS to know that they are not alone in their feelings, that others share the same fear, despair, and hope in their struggle. I am not the person with AIDS. I believe I can help, but the experience of other persons with AIDS is so important. Sometimes the group members would look to the workers as if to verify their information or feelings. I could verify the change in John, but his addressing the new member holds so much more importance for all of them.

Inviting Full Participation

To invite full participation is to selectively ask certain non-participants
to speak by looking at them or verbally seeking their comments. This
would be appropriate when more than two persons are present, some
are talking and some say nothing, and/or one or more persons seem to
dominate the communications.

Involving more than one person in making decisions is more complex than unilateral decision making. It is also more time-consuming.
However, to the extent that persons are part of the deciding, they are
apt to have greater commitment to the outcome and to pursue the
discussion's conclusions. The worker would invite full participation in
order to increase commitment, balance participation, and help each
person feel a part of the action. The following excerpt illustrates this
skill.

> This was an ad hoc parents' group that had been meeting weekly to
> raise money for athletic equipment which the high school needed.
> Most of the discussion for the last ten minutes was dominated by
> those who wanted the group to continue for six more weeks. I
> glanced around and asked if those who have not said anything
> would like to comment. This brought opinions from four others who
> had been watching quietly.

At times the social worker wants to search for a different voice
when she suspects people are merely being polite or following subtle
cultural expectations in situations where they would express themselves if they dared and such expression would make the work more
authentic. This can occur with couples or groups as the next situations illustrate.

In the example below, the social worker invites pull participation,
then universalizes.

> I met with Mr. and Mrs. Duncan to discuss how their experience as
> foster parents was going. They are new to the agency and are
> parenting their first child. Angie is ten years old and in her first
> placement since her parents separated last month. Her mother is
> unable to care for Angie and four younger children. Mr. Duncan

responded to my question of how things were going. He described in minute detail each day of the last ten days, at least those times when he was at home from work, five-thirty on. He minimized the difficulties and seemed intent on impressing me with how well they were all doing. I noticed that Mrs. Duncan looked at points as if she had other feelings. However, as he went on and on Mrs. Duncan did not interrupt. I looked at Mr. and then Mrs. I commented that I thought Mrs. Duncan seemed to want to put in her version of these days, and she was at home with Angie much of the day. Mrs. Duncan was quick to pick up on my lead and began discussing some of the fights they had, adding that she hoped things would go easier in time. I said beginnings were often tough. They smiled and nodded.

Sometimes cultural expectations move men to assume they must speak out and dominate the group. While many might really wish to be less vocal, they follow an unspoken norm that this would seem wimpish. In mixed gender groups this subtle expectation often leads men to take over in dealing with issues; and the women may collude in the arrangement by feigning passivity.[4] When this happens, as in the following instance, the social worker needs to invite full participation.

The social action committee of the Cherokee Neighborhood Association was planning how and where to have the victory party for the newly elected chair. James and Paul argued for several minutes about inner city versus suburban places. Richard cut in to talk about the menu; it should be elegant. John thought they should have two choices in case there were vegetarians in the group, as he was. Richard said this was out of the question for a group their size and it would be too expensive that way. I noticed all the women were sitting there, listening to the men arguing about the food. I said, "Only the men are talking. Would any of the women like to say something?" There was a pause in the excitement. Then Gladys said, "We have plenty of ideas. How about roast duck."

Turning Issues Back to the Group

A major objective of the social worker in working with groups is to help the participants take as much responsibility for their group life as possible. This imperative pilots the work regardless of group-type (e.g., committee, treatment, skill development). For some groups the movement is toward total autonomy and the worker moves into a consultative role with periodic contacts, or some "as needed" arrangement, or even total separation as the group moves to do its own guidance. In other instances the move toward self-direction may appear infinitesimal, and yet be movement.

The underlying concept here is *empowerment*.[5] The social worker aims to help the individuals toward increased control over their lives and to help the group generate its own agenda and priorities. The shift, as much as is possible, is from dependence upon the worker to independence or self-dependence. Underlying this skill are bedrock values of the social work profession: respect for the dignity of the individual, enhancement of self-determination, and belief in the importance of democratic decision-making.

Life learnings may reinforce one's sense of powerlessness, especially for many of social workers' clients whose place in the world is resourceless, precarious, debilitated, stigmatized, censured, or even despised. Mainly, the cultural surround of those who seek help from social workers has often worked against risk-taking, creativity, and independence. It has rewarded compliance behavior that neither makes waves nor rocks the boat. In many ways throughout one's life career, the learned message is to follow others' orders, to conform to others' expectations. And these messages grow more strident as the march toward specialization accelerates in the world of work.

Through numerous experiences, group participants may come to their groups conditioned to look to the worker for direction. This orientation may derive from childhood learnings in the family, school experiences, treatment by various "experts," or experiences in groups dominated by persons with a need to lead. It is sometimes seductive to fulfill the group participants' expectations; many professionals enjoy this "expert" status. On the other hand, for social workers a special expertise resides in knowing how to help group participants learn to take increased control of their destiny. They are helped to do this through the worker's turning issues back to the group.

To turn the issue back to the group is to ask the group participants to use their own experience and thinking to deal with speculations, problems, and plans, instead of avoiding working on these matters. The social worker turns the issue back to the group when more than two persons are present, the group seeks advice or direction from the worker, and she assumes the group has the background to deal with the issue itself. This response should occur whenever the group participants appeal to the worker and her supposedly superior knowledge and experience. In time the group will learn to anticipate such a response from the worker and begin to take more initiative in dealing with its problems and issues in its own way.

The following illustration of turning the issue back to the group happened in a support group of AMACs (Adults Sexually Molested as Children).

> This was our fourth session, and the women were having some difficulty in getting started. There was a period of silence. Then Gerry turned to me and said I should say something to help them get going. I looked around at all and said I was sure they could start things themselves when they felt like it. Gerry then said to the others that she had a good week and relayed some of her experiences. This got the ball rolling. Several commented on what Gerry talked about and added their week's experiences.

In the next situation, an outpatient veterans group dealing with alcoholism at a V.A. Hospital is embroiled with the issue of smoking or not during meetings.

> James turned to Larry, puffing away on his cigarette, and announced that Larry should go outside if he wanted to smoke; the room was too small for smokers. Bill spoke up and echoed James' sentiments, adding that it was unhealthy. Gabe, Len, and Joe hooted at the word "unhealthy." Robert said that if they were "healthy," they wouldn't be here in this group. Comments flew back and forth for several minutes. Larry defended himself and the others who wanted to smoke with two arguments: they have known enough restrictions in their lives without these added rules, and addicts

should be able to keep on with one addiction as they tried to stay off drinking. Joe agreed and lit up his cigarette in the excitement. The pros and cons continued heatedly when James turned to me for support for the no-smoking side. I said to James and the rest of the group, "The group will have to work out this problem so that everyone can live with the decision that gets made." The arguments subsided for a few seconds and there was some silence. Larry said that the meetings lasted only an hour. He thought that he and the other smokers should have a cigarette before the meeting in a nearby room and then go an hour without smoking. Silence. Joe said they might try this next week. They moved on then to other things.

Reaching for Consensus

To reach for consensus is to check to see if most of the participants are in agreement with how things are going. The social worker should reach for consensus periodically when more than two persons are present, when the communication is heated or lively, and when certain few participants seem to control the discussion.

Consensus is an ideal end to controversy and diversity among group participants.[6] It consists of a mutually agreed upon decision, often achieved by the participants' modifying their original perspectives or beliefs in order to come out with some solution that is acceptable to the whole group. Consensus may involve a compromise of certain prized sentiments on the part of various participants in the interest of group action and harmony. It is more easily achieved when group participants hold common values and have similar knowledge/ experience. This is a rare situation in organizations and in our pluralistic national culture where diversity abounds. Thus, we typically resort to majority/minority voting where some persons inevitably end up as the minority. Thus, reaching for consensus should be attempted before settling issues via voting.

In the following instance, the social worker is a supervisor in a family agency meeting with a planning committee of staff to consider in-service training.

Pat, Adrienne, and Dick had a lot to say about the speaker we had last week, mainly critical comments. <u>I turned to the others and asked whether they felt that way also.</u> All five offered different opinions. The discussion went back and forth and grew tense as two sides seemed to emerge, each sticking to its assessment. <u>I urged them to talk this over more so that we could get a collective notion about speakers for our next in-service events.</u>

In this same group the supervisor intervened again:

Noah and Mike thought the presentations at the agency were pitched to the lowest level of staff; they were boring and got in the way of the time spent with clients. Adrienne was glad, as a new worker, that the level was understandable to her. She added that some workers acted more elite than they ought to, glancing at Noah and Mike. On the defensive, Noah said some of them had their MSWs and should be valued rather than put down. Mike gave a little smile while Dick and Pat appeared sick of all this planning. Mike continued. He thought presentations should appeal to a sophisticated and innovative approach to the families or else they would continue to bore him. I said, "<u>We are taking the time here in talking and planning for the future so that the sessions will appeal to the whole staff. There are differences among staff as we all know and perhaps we can vary the focus of the in-services so that both newer and more experienced staff can connect with the content.</u>"

Reaching for Difference

A concomitant skill to reaching for consensus is reaching for difference.[7] In fact, consensus is meaningless if differences are forced underground in the interest of peacefulness. A satisfying resolution to differences, whether through consensus or voting, is all the more possible if differences are aired before a direction is taken. Participants in the group will feel all the more valued regardless of the outcome if they have had their time to wrestle with the issue, anticipate consequences, and view the situation from various perspectives. Then they are apt to be more committed to the group decision whatever it may finally be. They have had their day in court.

To reach for difference is to help the group participants see things from various angles, reviewing alternative points. If only positives are expressed, the social worker should elicit the opposite viewpoint. If only negative valuations are entertained, then the worker seeks expression of other possibilities. The worker helps the group see and think beyond dichotomies: right/wrong, yes/no, good/bad. In other words, the thinking and action may eventually involve shades and varieties of alternatives, and options for many possible outcomes. Reaching for difference is a means of combatting groupthink,[8] a tendency of group participants to strive for cohesiveness and concurrence with group pressure toward conformity or efficiency. Groupthink obscures the richness of diverse thinking.

The social worker reaches for difference when more than two persons are present, and the group's thinking seems to be biased or one-sided. In the following instance, the social worker reaches for difference when the whole group appeared to get down on one member.

The Parents Without Partners began to talk about Tom who was absent tonight. They seemed to want to use this opportunity to berate him and his loyalty to the group. I wondered if there might be some unexplained reason for his absence tonight. Sam remembered that Tom had talked about going out of town to visit his daughter this week. Adele thought that should certainly take precedence over this group, even though he did let us down by not bringing the information about restaurants as he had promised last week. Mike stopped his bad-mouthing and others started to try to make do without Tom's contributions.

10. Skills for Non-Talking Groups and Non-Talking Times with Groups

> I remember and I was.
> I feel and I am.
> I do and I become.
>
> Joan M. Erikson

In this chapter we focus on the doings of groups, on that portion of group life that is expressed in ways other than talking about something. And we look at how the social worker may get with and be with a group through communications in addition to speech. We shall revisit the continuous group skills presented in chapter 7 and the contingent group-building skills of chapter 8 in order to consider their application with non-talking groups (or those non-talking times in any group). Separating these non-talking skills from the other skills has been done in order to highlight them. The reader, however, must transport them into their functional place with the other skills (e.g., with selecting communication patterns, with voicing group achievements) in order to be ready to use them at appropriate times. We also introduce in this chapter new skills that are particularly suited to the *doing* realm: demanding expressiveness and building on strengths.

First, we must clarify what we mean by the non-talking group. It is not a silent group. Rather, it is a group that appears to be most at home when involved in activities. The activity is the driving force for whatever words are exchanged. The talk arises from the action, is about the action, and is mediated by it. Because of age-related experience, developmental needs, or special situations, some persons know what to do with each other as long as they are busy with play, with a project, or even with chores. These are the activity groups or groups that rely on doing things together during much of their meeting.

There are other considerations about non-talking groups. To see such groups as *non-talking* may really be a subtle instance of victim blaming. The group may *seem* to be non-talking to the would-be helper when really they talk well enough among themselves. Sometimes, the middle-class helpers—facile with words, report writing, and bureaucratic red tape—end up with a cultural gulf between them and those seeking help. They are perceived as foreign and frightening. It is almost as if the very process of gaining a professional education so alters the helpers that they grow unable to communicate simply with others in *their* realm. The assumedly non-talking group may through its silence be expressing resistance to unwanted services and workers. Or, the group members may have their own language which the worker doesn't understand, e.g., a foreign tongue, sign language, a teen or street jargon, a "secret" vocabulary. In such instances a shared activity might coax the reluctant group to chance an exchange with this new, strange person.

We think also about the various experiential approaches that have grown popular since the 1960s—the advent of the human potential movement with its encounter groups, marathons, skill development emphases, and the all-purpose "exercise." The general public is now familiar with varieties of interactional techniques. Even two-to-five-year-olds have been introduced to self-other social skills through planned activities.[1] Published directions now exist for activities dealing with values, with expressing feelings, developing team morale, working with women's and men's groups, and "everything you wanted to know about anything."[2]

Encounter techniques in the public schools are prevalent routes to teaching social-emotional, affective content along with the more academic content. Whole-person approaches to growth and learning, Eastern values, and different modalities of expression are directly known and valued now that right hemisphere brain workings are widely appreciated.

The legacy of the turbulent 1960s, especially for the unsettled and searching middle-class individual, included the explosive and ubiquitous group movement with its encounters and emphasis upon "letting it all hang out." Beyond this, there evolved the gradual, increased specialization in all the people-helping professions, including social work. By this we mean the route toward self-fulfillment grew more medicalized and psychologized for the worried or bored middle-class person. For those who made the community uncomfortable—the addict, the delinquent, the unemployed—the "in" approaches were more person-changing via behavior modification and various environmental controlling techniques. New professions emerged: activity directors for the nursing home, expressive therapists (the music therapist, dance therapist, etc.) for the hospital. Social workers concentrated more on talking and talk therapy, and eventually on being "clinical," thus leaving the activities and doing involvements mainly to the occupational, recreational, and expressive therapists.

We think this has been an unfortunate turn of events that now leaves many social workers unsure of how to connect with the schizophrenic or depressed person in the hospital or day treatment program, and unaware of the potentiality and value of work with others through what social group workers once called "program."[3]

We describe such work here in order to correct these blind spots and offer clues to how the social worker can work with groups in both the talking and doing modalities. We think singing, dancing, doing crafts, painting, cooking, and other such activities are not necessarily *therapy* simply because other professionals have claimed this turf. All of these pursuits *may be therapeutic*, just as vacations or reading are therapeutic. Or they may merely be the natural expressiveness all persons need to resort to periodically. The social worker can enter a communicative exchange through these realms and pursue her social work objectives in these modalities as needed.[4]

The primacy of talking, as contrasted with doing or experiencing in order to "know," is now eroded. Nonverbal communication is as important as verbal; doing is as important as talking for some persons. In fact, immersion in activities in which rules, order of performance, roles, and expected behavior are known to the participants may be thought of as the natural home of speech. What must be negotiated is the turns at talking!

In working with groups, social workers may communicate and structure interaction through various activities and *constructed* learning experiences.[5] These "constructions" include the guided fantasy, exercises, simulations, games, role plays, psychodrama, card playing, singing, ceramics, dance, and so forth. And social workers may join in the play of children, young persons, older adults, and all persons when they pursue what they know how to do—be it party, social, trip, or clean-up.

Sometimes the skills the social worker uses with non-talking groups involve entering the nitty-gritty affairs that are familiar to the group— the ordinary activities of everyday living. Such work is often painstaking and takes special patience to engage with the group participants on their own terms and turf and at their own pace. It involves entering what groups *do,* and through this helping them *become.* Thus the action and activities are learning media, are becoming-passports, are life. What groups do or produce link to the more sober requirements for valued participation in the world of affairs. These doings can link to competence, to self-value, and to connection with others.

The use of activities is suited to three major purposes. At the most basic level, activities can help the isolated, withdrawn, silent individual dare to approach another person, as when a usually mute mental patient in the hospital day room risks joining into a familiar song with the others during an evening sing-along. Second, they can help a person master the particulars needed to handle oneself with respect to others, the environment, and the world of ideas and tasks. This is learning "the rules of the game." Third, activities can help persons to move beyond this kind of coping-learning to innovation, and to develop their unique style of living. In other words, activities deal with matters of involvement, discipline, and creativity. They have to do with discovery—a process of inquiry into the world that exists, and with invention—a process of creating something entirely new.

Stage-Setting Skills

Recall the two stage-setting skills described in chapter 3, "engaging in the medium of the other" and "proposing a medium presumably congenial to the other." These also apply to communicating with groups. They are general, all-purpose actions that direct the worker to get with what the others are doing, or with what the social worker assumes the others would like to do.

Examples of "engaging" might be watching and then joining a game of pool with fellows who are involved in this, or meeting families of the "Association for the Mentally Ill" during the social part of their monthly program meeting, or having tea in the kitchen with the family of a hospice patient. Examples of "proposing the medium" to connect with a group include telling the boys who are hanging out near the office that you can take them for a ride to the shopping center in the van.

Continuous Group Skills

We now reconsider "thinking group," "scanning," and "fostering cohesiveness" from an activities perspective. In addition to the general "thinking group" concepts (e.g., roles, norms, communication pattern), there will be other concepts determined by the particular activity in which the group is engaged. The worker needs to be familiar with these particulars in order to understand what is going on. If the group is playing basketball, the worker must know about fouls, lay-ups, and so on. With other activities it is the same—one must "know the score."

Scanning also applies in non-talking group situations, only the range is broader, for the worker is not just sitting in the circle with the group. The activity of the moment may involve the participants in various configurations, e.g., at the ice-skating rink, on a hike, at a carnival. It becomes exceedingly critical for the social worker to see and know where each person is at all times.

Activities are inherently valuable for fostering cohesiveness. When groups participate along with other groups in any type of activity, in-group/out-group spirit is enhanced. For example, if several groups attend an outing, each group moves more within itself by virtue of the very overall arrangement. It is natural for the social worker to talk in terms of "our team," of "us" and of "them."

A special advantage of activities over talk is that all participants can be involved in the action at the same time. No one has to wait for a turn to say something. This is particularly useful for children, teens, beginning meetings, or ventures into little-known situations. Appreciating this, the worker may plan an activity as a way of helping a group get started.

Selecting Communications Patterns Purposely

The choice of an activity represents a special case of selecting communication patterns purposely. Activities are important especially when a communication barrier might exist between the social worker and the group participants. In the following instance, a white worker selects communication patterns purposely for meeting with a group of seven black, pregnant unmarried teenagers who came to E Hospital's outpatient clinic for supervision of their pregnancy.

> Aside from our essential humanness and femaleness, we were poles apart. They were frightened and resistant in response to this unplanned birth. They brought fears of the bodily changes of pregnancy and the unknown birth process, fear of physical pain, and fear of this hospital with its many unfamiliar procedures and personnel. They also feared isolation from their boyfriend and seemed reluctant to look at the social problem part, the non-physical part of their situation. I found them to be guarded, full of "yesses" and silences. They seemed willing to listen to what I wanted to say but not willing to get involved themselves.
>
> To move beyond this beginning stalemate, I ventured an approach which I thought might be more congenial to an interchange between them and me. I introduced a task explicitly related to their engagement with each other and with me in the context of the hospital at this particular point in their lives. It was to take action about the physical changes of pregnancy. At our first meeting I asked them to change out of their good clothes into the green surgeons' gowns. I was in this "costume" also. I then played soul music as a background and showed them some simple movements and exercises that I explained might help them in connection with pregnancy, birth, and relaxation.
>
> I constructed the movements to involve them with each other in pairs so as to begin to develop a supportive group culture. They were to hold hands, help their partner balance, watch their partner's progress, etc. They began to talk with each other, and then with me about how they were doing the exercises. . . . During a sitting-down time, I began to talk with them about what they eat and matters of nutrition.

In this instance the route to bridging the barrier between frightened young persons and a social worker who was strange to them was through the choice of a way of communicating with each other and her that was less threatening than talking—something they could do in unison rather than one-by-one.

In their second meeting, the social worker again selected a communication pattern so that work could proceed more easily than through just talk.

> We talked briefly about their exercises and whether or not they were able to continue with these at home. They were not very inclined to say anything. I had another task: I gave out some paper and pencils and asked them to draw a map that would show where they lived and how they got from their neighborhood to the hospital. They were in small groups of two or three so that they could talk with each other when they finished their map and find out more about each other, e.g., who comes on the subway? Who lives farthest away? This map was followed by another map that had to do with their shared present reality—the first floor of this hospital with the different people on it.

There are other ways through selecting communication patterns purposely that workers help newcomers to join a group or withdrawn individuals to make a connection with others. In the first instance, the social worker introduces an "ice breaker" or game-like activity that sweeps newcomers beyond their natural shyness in the new situation, e.g., the "Who Am I?" game in which the name of a famous person is pinned on each one's back and one tries to guess the name while milling about, introducing himself to others, and asking yes-or-no questions.

With the isolated person, the approach needs to be more subtle. Perhaps she will respond to doing something in pairs. The following example is such an instance. It was a drop-in center for transient and homeless women.

> After watching the patterns of the women who used the Center over several weeks, I noted some women preferred to sit alone, smoke a cigarette, and drink their coffee. Others watched the comings and goings and seemed approachable, even interested in having a con-

versation. There was always a cluster at the coffee urn. In time, I got to know the individuals who came daily and seemed possibly outgoing. I asked four of them if they might help with the way the Center worked, start a conversation with a newcomer? Take a toy (from a bagful I had collected from volunteers' contributions) and offer it to a woman with small children? My idea worked! Soon these "hostesses" took on the two tasks I suggested and connected with newcomers and family groups.

Voicing Group Achievements

We have described in chapter 8 the importance of the worker's acknowledging to the group their achievements whenever this is possible. She puts into words at the conclusion of a successful or satisfying experience what the group members might be feeling but not expressing. Sometimes, the participants might not even realize the achievement—too close to it, or unaware of their own progress. When the worker talks of what has been accomplished, group pride is enhanced and the individuals gain a sense of self-value. These remarks move the action from the feeling realm to the concept realm. The group is helped to claim its progress.

The next illustration is taken from a center for the physically disabled. Some of the participants are involved in the Sheltered Workshop where they learn to produce window shades and other household goods. The men here, however, are recently disabled and come to this group to meet others with comparable problems, begin to share feelings about their disability, and risk becoming more physically active. It has been hard to involve them in physical activity. Primarily they sit.

We were singing "The Bear Went Over the Mountain." I sensed they seemed to want to get out of their seats and attempted to make a singing game of the song by changing the words to "The Bear Went Around the Table." I introduced the song and the movements at almost the same time, trying to make the movement around the table relatively uncomplicated. They got up and moved around the room in a follow-the-leader form. They enjoyed this so much that they not only went around the tables, but out the door, around the hall, and back into the room. It was an activity that called upon some strengths they were not sure they had. They were smiling, but tired when they sank into their chairs. I commended them saying, "We've moved more this afternoon than ever before." They spontaneously began to clap for themselves.

Preserving Group History and Continuity

The residents of Friendship House are older adults who live in a low-income housing facility in a depressed inner-city area. There is an active nucleus of twenty-five to thirty persons here who like to meet each Tuesday in the Lounge for cards, talk, occasional lectures and concerts, and refreshments. They also take a monthly bus trip with their worker to various parks and nearby places of interest.

> After I had been on several outings with this group, I brought my Polaroid camera and took some pictures of the group on our visit to the zoo—boarding the bus, looking at the ducks in the pond, and eating at the picnic tables. At our next week's meeting I brought out a scrap book and the pictures. Mr. Toliver eagerly appropriated these and arranged them in the book. Then he appended date and place in his proud, bold handwriting. The group was delighted with their "memory book" and spontaneously discussed how they would add to it after each future trip. Mrs. Keen asked if it would be OK to put drawings in the book too. She would like to make some sketches on their outings. She got a lot of encouragement to do so. Spirits were running high.

Another instance of *preserving group history and continuity* is provided by a group of teen-age boys in a middle school who were part of the school social worker's group formed of potential drop-outs identified by their teachers as disruptive in the classroom.

> The guys were sullen and reluctant to come into the room. When they did come in and sit down, I could hear them using foul language under their breath, directing it toward everyone but me as I tried to talk about what we might do in this group. Then I hit upon an idea. I taped a long three-by-twenty-foot paper to the wall and

called it "The Graffiti Paper." I gave each of them a magic marker and encouraged them to go up to the paper and write their thoughts, or feelings, or problems on it (without adding their names). I said they should keep these markers and bring them to the meeting each week. Then I kept quiet and watched them gradually begin to fill up parts of the paper. A few doodles also appeared. After about fifteen minutes, I commended them for all this work and said we had enough to go on for several meetings. When we would finish an entry we would cross it off and go to another one. We tackled three problems the first session. They made a beginning sharing their troubles with each other.

Verbalizing Norms

For some groups the underlying concept of norms—what it is OK and not OK to do in the group—is best approached through working out and adhering to the rules of a game. For example, a social worker helped a group of nine-to-twelve-year-old foster children in a group home for emotionally disturbed boys set up and deal with some rules for baseball. They came up with the following:

1. Although no one is forced to play, those who choose to do so must follow the rules.

2. No foul language or the player is out of the game.

3. There must be an inning limit determined in advance. You just don't play until it is dinner time and those who are ahead then win. You know at the outset how many innings you are going to play. And if, in the last inning the first team at bat is still behind after its batting, you don't play out the last half inning. There is already a winner. You stick to the rules.

4. If one member of the team quits, he is out for the whole game.

5. All balls and strikes are called. No extra chances. Batting order must be followed.

6. You must follow the direction of your captains and the rulings of the umpire (worker), however unfair they may seem to be.

7. The pitcher must stay in his box. There are no running leads from first base. Wild pitches bring a walk to the batter.

Over time, the boys learned to live with these rules which the worker, as umpire, pointed out whenever enforcement was necessary. Through sticking with their rulings in the game, the boys were learning to develop impulse control, consideration of others, and cooperation with their teammates.

In the instance below, the worker reminds the group members of a norm they had established. It is at an auction which a booster group of parents of children with hemophilia were holding at the county fair.

> Mrs. James, Mrs. Clark, and Mrs. Trumbel were angry at Mrs. Martin, the auctioneer, because she was rushing too fast before everyone had a chance to bid on an item. Mrs. Martin was nervous in her role and seemed flustered by the disapproving faces the others made at her. Nevertheless, she kept on as she was doing, talking faster in fact. I whispered to the three "helpers" that we had decided last week to move briskly at the start in order to involve a large audience. They seemed calmed by this reminder.

We can see the social worker in the following situation *verbalizing norms* with institutionalized schizophrenic patients around the activity of the afternoon snack in the hospital day room.

> I had initiated having refreshments, sodas, and cup cakes, on Tuesday afternoons at three o'clock in advance of our community meeting. Jerry sat in his chair mumbling and looking at the floor. Frank laughed and rushed to the table. Marie stood by the door. Phyllis and Margaret looked at me and then slowly approached the table; they said they wanted donuts and not cupcakes and started to grab for the cans. I reminded them that we knew there was enough for each of us and we needed to start with only one cake and the kind of soda we liked. I then asked Phyllis to pass around the plate of cakes to each person, and Frank to distribute plates and napkins. They seemed to calm down and waited to be served. After, I asked Phyllis to see who wanted seconds. I heard some thank you's and told them so, and that this was the way we were getting used to serving and having the snack. I added that they said they wanted

donuts. We could be sure to have these for our snack tomorrow. Would they like to have donuts?

Encouraging Development of Traditions and Rituals

The following episode shows how one worker was able to help a group develop a way of ending each meeting that also helped them move toward greater responsibility for their work together.

> The six seventeen-year-old girls in foster care that I called together to form a group for beginning to prepare for independent living had been meeting for two months. They gradually developed some bond with each other and seemed to be following through with the tasks that were outlined in each session. But they still were mainly passive and relied on me to present the focus and plans for each meeting. I told them of my view that this was a problem, that they were just sitting back and I hoped they would begin to take more responsibility for the content of the group meetings. However, this information didn't seem to arouse them.
>
> At the next meeting I tried another approach. I proposed that we should now begin to end each meeting in the following way: we would put on a tape recording of a tune of their choice and while this played, we would pass a pencil around the circle from one to another, being careful not to drop it. Then, when the song ended, that person with the pencil would take the responsibility for picking out the focus for next week's meeting. This seemed to appeal to them. There was some laughter and they said they would start this today. (The idea was successful and became the way we ended each meeting thereafter).

Banana Splits is an innovative peer support group approach to children who share feeling of loss and change as a result of separation, divorce, or life in single parent or remarried families. According to the program's founder, the name *Banana Splits* reflects who the youngsters and teens are, and is part of the reason for this program's success. The children are "up" kids, living in a crazy situation, but surviving, and surviving well for the most part. *Banana Splits* makes a positive statement: the love of ice cream is a child's birthright; and

Splits conveys the reality that the families have split up. The message is clear: "This is not a group to be pitied. . . . Their self-image as a group is positive to themselves and to the world. . . . [much better as a name than] 'Kids of the Separation and Divorce' group."[6]

So much for the power of names as important organizing symbols and attractions with image appeal! The following view of a social worker meeting weekly with elementary school children shows the *development of tradition and ritual* as important "glue" that enhances the impact of the group on its participants:

> I made a large construction paper logo, a banana tree, that reached from floor to ceiling, and taped it to the wall. When the children came for the first time, I asked them to draw and cut out their own bananas to put on the tree. They should also put their name on their banana before attaching it to a branch. The tree produced a very quick image to all the children that they were not alone. We save and use this tree as a prop each time we meet, and when a new child comes, the others are quick to have him make and add his banana.

Demanding Expressiveness

At times the doing activities are valuable simply because they impel a group to action that would not have happened otherwise. Recall the disabled men moving into the hall and back as "The Bear Went Around the Table"! Or the sullen boys' group at school writing their problems on the graffiti paper. Or the pregnant young women exercising in their green surgeon's gowns. These situations were described for other purposes. But in each case there was some "magic" to the activity that helped the worker and group start a process of working together.

Perhaps it is the playfulness involved, or the connection with happier times, or the change from serious affairs and worries. Or is it the humor? The call for spontaneity? The juxtaposition of difference into a situation where it is least expected? Or all of these things!

For whatever the reasons, activities that are thoughtfully proposed as potentially interesting (and age, class, culture, and gender appropriate) can link to untapped realms and transport the group and its participants to a new, different space. And in this experience new "voices" may be expressed that have not been heard before.

We stress the importance of thoughtfulness on the part of the worker. No "cook book mentality" that plunges a group into "exercises" that do violence to a group's natural process. Older adults, for example, should not be infantilized by having them play child-like rhythm instruments. But they might be involved with actual musical instruments, or accompany recorded music with adult percussion materials. Or they might revisit earlier times through familiar danceable music. The activity or task that is proposed by the worker must fit the competencies of age and other aspects of the groups' background. Activities are a desired form of communication for young children. The congenial activity for all others requires careful selection.

The following episode is from a rehabilitation center for the physically handicapped. Often these patients are the victims of a sudden traumatic experience—accident, paralysis—that almost annihilates their sense of who they are as persons. They are shocked by their new limitations and by their dependence on others for even the simplest activities of living. They are among the most difficult challenges to the workers so far as expressiveness is concerned. We see here how the worker interjects activity to *demand expressiveness*.

> I brought the tape recorder to the fourth floor recreation room and set it at the table where Mr. Arnold and Mr. Mason were. Mr. Mason was a patient who never came to any group activity because he was so afraid of groups of people. But he took an interest in the tape recorder and not only stayed but participated during the entire program. At my urging, both Mr. Mason and Mr. Arnold said a few words into the recorder and I then played back the tape so that they could hear their voices. As other patients appeared and came over to see what was going on, Mr. Rosen began to speak into the recorder and got Mr. Mason to talk. They were glad to hear their voices played back to them. . . . After I had read one story where they were to fill in the blanks with ideas from TV commercials, we had the playback. Several funny words and phrases had been given by the patients. Everyone was now participating and the atmosphere was

relaxed. Before reading another story, I asked if anyone else would like to try something. Mr. Johnson asked if he could sing a song. He sang a rousing spiritual. <u>I began to clap. Soon several others joined me in clapping their hands to the beat.</u>

Building on Strengths

The last skill we consider in this chapter is specially pursued in the other-than-talk arena: building on strengths. If we adopt a whole-person perspective and look beyond the person-with-a-problem to see all that the person *knows* and *can do,* new vistas appear. The alienated ones, the "hard to reach," the homeless, the struggling single parent, the unmarried teenager with two children—they have something going for them that needs to be appreciated. They must have strengths in order to survive as well as they do in the hard situations they must face. What is it they know? What can they show us if given the chance?

How to manage from the thrift shops? To use newspaper coupons strategically? To rear the children in the midst of chaos? To vary the meals on next to nothing? To live in cramped quarters, often with several families? To give and take? To retain some optimism?

Perhaps the spark is there if the worker can just find and connect with it, can focus on what they know how to do and *have* accomplished. Perhaps the connection through which the worker reaches them will come through a shared interest or activity that can be maximized with the worker's help. It is this kind of possibility that the following episode illustrates.

At the Riverview Nursing Home I tried to orient new residents through several intake interviews during their first two weeks. My objective was to acquaint them with some of the living routines, prepare them for sharing a bedroom if necessary, and connect them with other "seasoned" residents who might look out for them. This worked much of the time, but not when things got hectic, and neither I nor the others followed through with a newcomer. I decided to share "my" problem. I started a group for volunteer residents who would meet Tuesday afternoons and deal with matters of orientation. As things developed, there were about seven regulars who named themselves The Welcome Ones. They reviewed their own entrances and worked out a list of daily attentions they would offer newcomers. What seemed especially interesting was their response to my question, "What can you do to help the newcomers feel good about themselves in these new surroundings and tell something about themselves to you?" There was a pause. Then Dora said she could bring her embroidery with her and show it, and see whether the new person liked it and had things of her own that she could show. This stimulated lots of ideas: the knitting, the special recipes, the photos of one's family, and so on . . . The group began to meet new residents this way. They were proud of their achievements and also did a good job of helping newcomers settle in.

In the next instance, a worker helped a group enhance its own sense of competence through calling attention to their strengths.

I met with the newly developing Huntington's Disease group in response to their request that they needed a social worker. So far, this was a collection of about twenty persons who had found a meeting room in a local agency and had some organizing suggestions from the H.D. organization in another city. Their first few once-a-month meetings featured various speakers: a neurologist from a nearby university, a person trained in an Alzheimer's support group, a social worker from a family agency. The group formed itself around these informational meetings.

They called me because they wanted more than just information and they knew I knew something about groups. I volunteered to help them. Actually, I found three groups squeezed together in a small, smoke-filled room: the patients, their spouses or care givers, and those at risk (family members who may or not develop the disease). I helped the groups plan for different agendas and for the care givers to meet at an extra session each month so that they could become the support group for each other that they needed to be.

One theme I readily discovered was the lack of community support, and of professional knowledge about their disease. Even most physicians were unknowing of the particulars of the problem. There was much story telling of how the various individuals through trial and error had to learn how to manage: with physical arrangements for the home, with working the financial assistance system, with transportation, and so forth. As they swapped these tales, I was impressed with their collective fund of knowledge and told them so. "Why don't you make a book of your know-how? You know more about this disease than anyone in this city—about the disease itself, the management challenges, the resources, the specialists who have helped you, and so forth." They jumped at this. They had not sensed their expertise. They began their "encyclopedia" at the next meeting and have kept enlarging it at each meeting. Incidentally, this project has also served to engender a cohesiveness and cooperative spirit among the members.

PART FOUR

Strategic Skills

11. Skills for Dealing with Barriers

> "Speak when you're spoken to!" the Queen sharply interrupted her.
> "But if everybody obeyed that rule," said Alice, "and if you only spoke when you were spoken to, and the other person always waited for *you* to begin, you see nobody would ever say anything."
>
> Lewis Carroll

There are times when a client is unable to speak directly or speak at all about particular ideas. Sometimes the idea threatens to overwhelm the client with unwanted affect. Sometimes the idea is socially unacceptable. Sometimes it is taboo. Sometimes it feels as if saying something could jeopardize the client's status with the worker. Sometimes the client is prevented from speaking by dominant or disturbing others. Sometimes there are racial, ethnic, gender, or social class differences that inhibit or otherwise interfere. In any of these instances, work could be interrupted. Whatever interrupts the progress of the work can be considered a barrier requiring worker attention and intervention.

It should be noted here that there is nothing inherently worthwhile in dealing with barriers. The social worker addresses barriers solely in order to temporarily inactivate or remove them so that purposeful work can begin or continue.

Skills for dealing with barriers include referring to purpose, opposing defenses, pointing out resistance, challenging blocks, breaking taboos, and bridging differences.

Referring to Purpose

To refer to purpose is to re-state the reason client(s) and worker came together. This behavior is used when the client or clients seem to have strayed from the previously agreed-upon foci for meeting together.[1]

When the social worker refers to purpose, she tells the client(s) that there is a difference between what we (worker and client or clients) said that we were going to do and what we seem to be doing. There are times when this act is sufficient to remove a barrier temporarily and permit work to resume. Use of this behavior is illustrated in the following example.

> Treena told me that she finally told her husband, Richard, that she didn't want him to criticize her anymore, that she never criticizes him and that she would like him to reciprocate. She said he responded by asking her if she wanted him to pretend instead of being honest. "A statement like that can put you in a real bind," I said. She nodded, then started to tell me about an incident that had occurred between her father and mother. I listened for a while, thinking there was a connection between her parents' episode and her situation which we were talking about, but then she started talking about her niece and nephew in an entirely different kind of situation. I said, "Treena, we said we were going to work on your talking up for yourself with Richard, but we don't seem to be focusing on that right now." "I guess we better get back to it," she said, "because I can't handle it by myself. Once he said that to me— about pretending or being honest—I was stuck for an answer."

In the next example, a social worker refers to purpose in order to begin the work that members of a mental health center task force had previously agreed they needed to do.

> After the four chiefs of service and I arrived for the meeting to work out details for shortening the intake procedure, there was a lot of talk about different patients, Dr. Bradley's wife, and other extraneous subjects. I waited about five minutes and then said that we had agreed to meet to work out a plan for shortening the intake procedure, but that we didn't seem to be doing that.

Opposing Defenses

A defense is a mental mechanism for protecting against danger aris-
ing from one's own impulses or affects. It can be thought of as a
device for coping with stress from inside the self. Like coping devices
in general, when defenses are adaptive, they are valuable. It is necessary for the social worker to oppose them only when their use protects
the client's feelings at the expense of the work she is trying to do.

In the following example, a woman who was molested as a child
struggles with her rules for sexual behavior. Initially, she rationalizes
and the social worker opposes this defense. When her efforts to rationalize fail, she uses another defense, projection. So the social worker
opposes her projection, as well.

> "You know," said Marion, "I stopped sleeping around several months
> ago, but there's a big medical conference coming up, and when I'm
> out of town at a conference . . . you know, in a conference hotel . . .
> it's different. It's not like picking up strangers. These are men in the
> same profession I am." "Even if you never met them before they're
> not strangers?" I asked. "That's right," she replied. "Then what
> makes a person a stranger?" I asked. "Well," she began, then stopped.
> I waited. There was a long silence. Then she said, somewhat an-
> grily, "You think you can see right through me, but you can't!" "No"
> I said, "I don't think I can see through you, but apparently you think
> I can see through you!" There was another long silence.

Pointing Out Resistance

Unlike defense, which is intrapsychic, resistance is interpersonal. It
refers to the client's reluctance to talk about something in the client-
worker relationship.[2] Often, the *something* that is left unsaid can get
in the way of the work.

Clients resist making direct statements about anything that might
be construed as negative in the client-worker relationship because
they fear jeopardizing their vulnerable status with the worker. They
resist for fear that what they are thinking may displease the worker

and result in the worker's angry retaliation. They resist mentioning things that may offend the worker and lead her to do less than her best for the client. This happens, among other reasons, because the client feels dependent upon the goodwill of the worker. Therefore, when clients avoid discussing their implicit attitudes and feelings toward, or ideas about, the worker (whether real or transferential), and such avoidance seems likely to hinder the work that the client and the worker came together to do, the social worker should point out resistance.

To point out resistance is to state what is going on in the client-worker situation that the client is unwilling to say.

In the following example, the social worker points out resistance when a man seeking help seems unwilling to talk.

> For at least twenty minutes, Alan who was very talkative in our initial session last week, had very little to say. Then I remembered that something he talked about last week could be operating between him and me, so I said, "Alan, what you told me last week about the woman in the waiting room who had three different workers in four months might make you reluctant to start telling me anything significant." He smiled with some embarrassment and shrugged, saying, "Not much sense in talking about stuff when workers constantly leave the agency."

In the next example, the clue to resistance is the client's indirect reference to the client-worker situation, along with a facial expression toward the worker appropriate to the outside situation described. Thus the worker points out resistance.

> Jackie, a young black woman, told me that she is very angry at the office manager where she works as a secretary because the woman treats her as if she is dumb. She said the woman lectures to her, explains things three and four times, and sometimes even asks her to repeat back the instructions. Then she sat back and glared at me. I said, "What you just told me about the white woman who treats you like you are dumb is something like what you feel is going on between us, but you're reluctant to say so." "What makes you think that?" she asked. "Because you were glaring at ME the whole time you talked about it," I replied. She laughed. "I do get pissed off at

you for stuff like that sometimes," she said, still grinning. "<u>Well
next time I piss you off like that, would you tell me if you can?</u>" I
asked. She nodded, then added, "If I can."

Challenging Blocks

Sometimes some of the rules for social behavior that people have
learned can block the work that needs to be done. An injunction
against discussing family business outside the home, for example, can
hinder worker-client efforts to facilitate an adolescent's identity struggle. An injunction against raising one's voice can result in group
decisions made without one's input when excitement builds and with
it the voices of members not similarly constrained. A belief that consequential decisions should be made by men can deprive a family of
the wisdom of its female members. When such injunctions or beliefs
block discussion of relevant content or interfere with the appropriate
process of the work, it is important for the social worker to challenge
the block.

When the social worker knows what is getting in the way of the
work, she can challenge the block by indicating that something has
gotten in the way of the work, pointing out what the obstacle appears
to be, and initiating discussion of it. When the worker does not know
what has gotten in the way, on the other hand, she can indicate that
something has, and ask the client to speculate with her about what
may be interfering.

It should be noted that a belief or an injunction is usually linked to
other beliefs and injunctions in a larger system that guides the person's interactions with the world of people and events. Thus worker-
client discussion of a particular belief or injunction as an obstacle to
the work at hand should be understood as situation specific. It must
be clear that the worker is not asking the client to abandon his rules,
but rather, to temporarily suspend the ones that are currently hinder-
ing the work which the client and the worker jointly agreed to do.

In the following example, the social worker challenges a block
posed by the client's idea of proper behavior toward an expert, and at
least for the moment, the client moves beyond the obstacle and work
resumes.

Mr. Flynn came for help controlling his teenage son's behavior. Since Mrs. Flynn's death last year, Kenny started acting up in school, and recently he's been in trouble with the police, too. In our last two sessions, Mr. Flynn enthusiastically welcomed my suggestions and we agreed he'd try them out. But last week and this week he reported that he had not done so though he didn't know what prevented him from doing it. So I said that maybe my suggestions weren't really suitable for him and his son. He denied this, telling me I was right on target. Then I told him that I knew that sometimes people figure that they should listen to experts and not question them or tell them how their own situations don't fit what the expert is talking about. I waited. After several seconds he said that he knew my idea about telling Kenny that teenagers sometimes get angry when a parent dies and encouraging Kenny to talk about it was exactly what needed to be done, but that he can't talk about his wife without crying, and he won't let Kenny see him cry. "It can be very hard to talk when you've got so much feeling going on inside of you," I said.

Breaking Taboos

Personal and social taboos exist to protect one's self, society, or both, from the shame, guilt, and embarrassment that accompany encounters in highly sensitive areas of social and personal concern. When such personal or social taboos prohibit the mention of feelings and behaviors pertinent to the task at hand or the situation in which work on the task proceeds, these taboos become obstacles to task accomplishment. Such taboos must be broken by the social worker if the work is to continue.[3]

To break a taboo, the social worker mentions what is for the client unmentionable. By mentioning the unmentionable, the potency of the taboo can often be reduced for a while, permitting the work to resume.

In the following example, the social worker breaks a taboo by mentioning the unmentionable—that the client is, in fact, handicapped.

I was to have my third meeting with Steve at 7 p.m., and once again he was fifteen minutes late. When I confronted him with his constant lateness he apologized, saying that the only available parking spaces at this time of night were several blocks away. Steve, a cerebral palsy victim, wears a leg brace and walks slowly. I said that he didn't have to park so far away; that there are handicapped parking spaces right by the front door. He looked at me like I was crazy. "Steve," I said, "You are entitled to use the handicapped parking spaces right next to the door." He said that they are not for him, that he's just like everyone else, that his parents and his teachers always told him that and that that's what he believes. I said he may be like everyone else in most ways, but that he is handicapped when it comes to walking at a an average speed for an adult. I also said that it wasn't fair of him to pretend that he wasn't at my expense, that I have had to wait fifteen minutes for him all three times we had appointments. I said that he could be here on time if he used the handicapped parking spots to which he is entitled.

The behavior of the worker thus far may seem somewhat harsh and self-centered. She is not accepting and encouraging of a man whose struggles are many and whose willingness to struggle speaks to the great depth of his strength. But *unnecessary* struggling is neither virtuous nor pragmatic. And praise for unnecessary struggling is condescending.

The social worker does not patronize her *able* client, and as is seen below, the client examines for the first time in his life the way in which his taboo regarding the word 'handicapped' has kept him frightened. Ultimately, through several further sessions with the social worker, the client recognized that via the taboo, he had been depriving himself of rights to which he is entitled. He now exercises his rights.

"I never thought of myself as handicapped before," he said. "Then it can hurt to hear me say it now," I replied. "It scares me," he said. "If I think of myself that way I might use it as an excuse to not do well in school or at work. I only do well because I believe there's nothing I can't do." "You make it sound like magic, Steve," I said. "Actually, you do well in school and at work because you are intelligent and you work hard." "Yes," he acknowledged, "but maybe I wouldn't work as hard if I let myself believe I'm handicapped." "Is that what's so scary about the word <u>handicapped</u>"? I asked. He nodded and there were tears in his eyes.

Bridging Differences

There are sometimes differences between clients and workers, differences in age, gender, race, religion, social class, economic class, and so forth, and these differences sometimes become barriers to the helping process.[4] Troubled teenagers often imagine that adults could never understand or appreciate their struggles. Often black clients doubt that white workers could know what it is like for them. And women tend to wonder how men could understand the horror of such deliberate atrocities as rape and spouse abuse. When awareness of such categorical differences as these seem to create the sort of distance between client and worker that hinders the work needing to be done, the social worker must try to bridge the difference and close the distance.

To bridge a difference the social worker reaches across the invisible line between herself and the client by indicating that the worker is aware of the difference, aware that the client is aware of and probably feels the difference, and that this difference, if not talked about, could get in the way. Sometimes this, in and of itself, is sufficient to bridge the difference temporarily and permit meaningful work to ensue. Sometimes it is necessary for the social worker to go one step further and suggest that, because the outcome of the work is important to the client, it may be worth risking the necessary time, energy, and disclosure in the hope that help as the client would define it might actually occur.

It should be noted that the going one step further described above does not include injunctions to "trust me" or "trust the process." People cannot simply trust workers who are relative strangers to them, especially in the face of categorical differences that carry with them a history of misunderstanding. Nor should people be encouraged to trust in such situations. Trust increases vulnerability, and clients are already too vulnerable. Besides, they just won't do it, and all the worker who says "trust me" accomplishes is to fool him/herself into thinking trust has been established.

In the following example, the social worker bridges a difference that could be a barrier if it were not openly addressed.

"Look, Mr. Cook, I know you think I'm a nice kid and that you like me," I said. "I do like you," he confirmed. "But you know I'm too young to have experienced what you go through every day!," I said. Silence. "And you may even figure that a kid like me can't help you." Silence. "Right?" I continued. A nod. "But you want to get out of this depression real bad, don't you." I said. "I sure do," he said. Then he sighed and added, "I'm probably being foolish. You youngsters are right out of school with the latest techniques. I guess I'd just be more comfortable talking to someone closer to my own age. But here I am already talking to you, aren't I? So I guess I already decided to try it out with you." I nodded. "How about if anytime you feel uncomfortable, you say so and every time I think you may be a little uncomfortable I'll say so?" I suggested. "It's a deal," he said.

12. Skills for Coping with Conflict

> Tweedledum and Tweedledee
> Agreed to have a battle;
> For Tweedledum said Tweedledee
> Had spoiled his nice new rattle.
> Just then flew down a monstrous crow,
> As black as a tar-barrel
> Which frightened both the heroes so,
> They quite forgot their quarrel.
>
> Lewis Carroll

At times, people who come to see social workers are desperate for services and angry that they cannot receive them either immediately or at all. At times, people who come to see social workers are infuriated by their ill treatment at the hands of countless inexperienced clerks and overworked professionals. At times, social workers must tell people things they are loathe to hear—that their fourteen-year-old child is using drugs, that an anonymous caller has alleged that they have abused their children. At times, frazzled supervisors blow up at workers when they cannot find all the workers' reports which they need in order to compile summaries required by their own supervisors by a particular deadline date. In situations like these, conflicts occur, and situations like these are inevitable and ubiquitous. Therefore, social workers need skills for coping with conflict.

Five skills that help social workers cope with conflict are confronting situations, validating angry feelings, focusing on facts, converting arguments into comparisons, and proposing superordinate goals.

Confronting Situations

The term confrontation often arouses anxiety, for it conjures up images of angry persons shouting nasty remarks at each other. This unfortunate association seems to have had its genesis in the 1960s with the popularized notion that inhibition was bad and that the encounter group, versions of which sprang up all over the place, was *the* painful but powerful route to self-knowledge, sensitivity, and interracial understanding. None of these goals were achieved through such an attack oriented technique, however, and, although some alcohol and drug abuse programs still use this technique, it has for the most part been abandoned. But confrontation continues to carry negative overtones.

A more appropriate use of the term confrontation, and the way it is used here, implies a straightforward, civil presentation of descriptive information. The intent is to involve relevant persons in an open exchange of information and affect about a problem as each participant perceives it. The aim of such confrontation is to work through differences and arrive at a solution that is as optimal as possible for all of the persons concerned. To engage in this process, the social worker need not, indeed must not, shout, argue, or otherwise seem ready to do battle. In fact, the skill of concern here is confronting *situations*, for it is far more productive to confront situations with people than it is to confront people.

To confront a situation, tell the other person, *"We* have a problem," then make a straightforward, declarative statement that provides the essential information. The appropriate attitude for the social worker is one of openness, honesty, and genuine concern for both the situation and the other person. The worker's operating assumption is that the other person will care about the situation and want to work toward resolving the problems involved.

In the following example, a school social worker goes to the home of a ninth-grade student in order to confront a situation.

When Mr. Thomas answered the door, I said, "Mr. Thomas?" to make sure I was talking to the right person. He nodded and said yes. Then, with a very sober look on my face, I said, "I'm Ellen O'Conner, the social worker at Billy's school, and you and I have a problem. Billy has been caught selling drugs out of his locker." Mr. Thomas looked stunned. "He's what? Mother of God! Where is he? Is he okay?" he asked all at once. "He's okay and he's at school," I said. "May I come in so we can talk about what's going on and what we can do to help?" He stood aside to let me by.

In the next example, a social worker confronts a situation with a colleague.

"Judd," I said, walking into his cubicle. "There's something we have to deal with." "You and me?" he asked? I nodded. "What?," he asked. "My clients can hear you when you laugh, and some of them think you're laughing at them. Mr. Baker, the guy who just left, said me and my buddy next door ought to find his case file a real knee-slapper," I said sadly. "Hey, man," Judd said with real concern, "I'm not laughing at them!" I nodded. "But they don't know that," I said.

Validating Angry Feelings

Sometimes people are sent to social workers against their will. Frustrated parents and teachers send the teenagers whose behavior baffles and upsets them. Judges "sentence" drunk drivers to "counseling." When such involuntary clients arrive, they are often angry. Sometimes, too, social workers have to say things to clients that tend to arouse anger in them. But whatever the reason behind the feeling, it is difficult, if not impossible, to involve angry people in joint efforts to explore problems and work toward resolving them in a rational way. Thus, when faced with an angry person, the social worker's first task is to reduce the anger.

Statements most likely to reduce anger are not those that offer explanations or appeals to reason. Rather, it seems that anger responds best to recognition and validation, to statements that acknowledge the anger and indicate that it is justified.

In the following example, a school social worker validates the angry feelings of a parent whose son was suspended for drinking alcohol in school.

I came in at 7:30 a.m. to meet with Mrs. Dawson so she could get to her job by 9:00, and when I arrived, she was already standing outside my office door. "Coming here is a tremendous inconvenience for me," she said angrily as we walked in. "Yes," I responded, "it's very hard for working mothers to come to school." "It certainly is," she said. "By not getting to work until 9:00 today, I'm losing an hour's pay!" "No wonder you're angry!" I said. "You're the sole support of your family, and an hour's pay is a lot to forego!" "You bet it is," she said. "And on top of that," I added, "You're probably worried about Douglas's drinking." She nodded. "That's why I'm losing an hour's pay to come here," she said in a quieter voice. "I don't know what to do besides ground him for two weeks—which I did." "Maybe we can work together on it," I offered. "We've been putting together an Ala-Teen Chapter. . . ."

In the example below, a social worker validates the angry feelings of a man who was "sentenced" to counselling for drunk driving.

Mr. Brooks came in looking disgusted. "Hi," I said, "you look like you'd like to be any place but here." "That's right," he said, with the same disgusted look. I motioned him to a nearby chair and I sat in the one at right angles to him. "What happened?" I asked. He told me, with a lot of anger, about how the police stopped him just about a block from the club where he was at. He said they were laying for people coming out of that club, and that when they stopped him, they gave him a breatholizer test. He said he was just a hair over the legal limit, and boom, they took him in. "That can be real hard to take," I said, "being so close to the legal limit and all." "Yeah," he responded. "Well, the lousy judge said I showed 'poor judgment.' " He pooched his lips out, deriding the phrase. "Then he told me I could go get counseled or go to jail." "And being nobody's fool, you picked counseling, right?," I said with a half-way grin. "Here I am," he said with a big grin. "So what are we going to talk about?"

At that point I figured we could try getting down to business, so I started telling him some of the things I can help people with.

Focusing on Facts

As indicated above, when the social worker confronts situations or gives people information that evokes anger in them, it is necessary to reduce their anger so that joint problem-solving can take place. And in such instances, the reduction of anger is best accomplished by validating it. When the social worker is being confronted by an angry person, on the other hand, instead of validating the anger, the worker should focus on facts.

Focusing on facts requires sorting fact from emotion, then taking in and retaining the facts the other person presents in order to do what needs to be done. Given that in conflict situations emotions of both self and other tend to run high, facts taken in need to be checked for accuracy and retention should not be left to the vagaries of memory. Rather, the social worker should write them down. It is usually helpful, in terms of accuracy, to ask the other person to repeat what she or he has just said so that the worker can accurately record the substance of it. From an accurately recorded concern or set of concerns, the worker can look into or do whatever it is that dealing with the concerns requires.

It should be noted that there are added advantages to writing down the other person's concern. For one thing, writing provides an alternative to reacting in the heat of the moment, at that critical point where an emotional reaction could well fuel the other person's anger rather than reduce it. Also, the worker can avoid becoming defensive or arguing, both of which tend to prolong non-productive conflict. In writing down what the other is saying, the social worker's message is that what the other has said is worth careful thought, and that the worker will act on it.[1]

Along with the above, there is frequently a happy by-product from asking the other person to repeat so that the worker can write down what is being said. In repeating the statement, more slowly because writing is slower than the pace of normal speech, the speaker tends to say it with less emotion than accompanied its initial expression, and this is generally a relief to both the speaker and the listener.

In the following example, a social worker focuses on facts when angrily confronted by his supervisor. Notice that the worker's focus on facts helps both persons to focus on facts.

Mr. Russell came into my office practically shouting, "The Broadtree case file is three months behind. Wagner is four months behind. How am I supposed to review placements without information? And where's your itemization for the reimbursement amount you submitted last week?" I quickly grabbed a tablet and pen and began writing. As I wrote, I checked the facts. "Broadtree," I said, "is that the file that's three months behind?" "Yes," he said angrily, "and —" "What was the name of the second file?" I interrupted.

"Wagner," he said a little more softly. "The Wagner file is four months behind. I wrote it as he said it. "And the third item is my itemized list of expenditures for last week's request for reimbursement?" I asked, writing that down also. "Yes," he said calmly. "Broadtree, Wagner and itemization," I summarized for both of us. "I'll have it on your desk by four-thirty this afternoon. "OK," he said, leaving. "Good."

Converting Arguments Into Comparisons

Arguments are rarely productive and often create bad feelings that continue to haunt interpersonal relationships long after the arguments themselves have ended. To minimize the potential antagonism and hostility which arguments generate, the social worker can convert arguments into comparisons. This is done by re-interpreting or reframing the different sides of the argument as differences of opinion about the way in which to accomplish a particular end or goal which they both want. The sides of the argument then become options for consideration, comparison, and discussion among rational and concerned persons.[2]

In the following example, a social worker at a group home for delinquent boys converts arguments among staff members into comparisons.

After an incident that was mishandled by the three houseparents on the four to midnight shift, the Houseparent Supervisor, Mrs. Teller, the Program Supervisor, Mrs. Magee, and I got together to figure out what to do. Mrs. Magee was adamant about firing them all, while Mrs. Teller was equally adamant about giving them a suspension instead.

In an angry voice, Mrs. Teller told Mrs. Magee that whatever happens, her answer is always to get rid of the houseparents, and since the houseparent staff was predominantly black, it's "blame the blacks and get rid of them!" Mrs. Magee said icily that she resented the implication that she was a racist, but would overlook it. She said that the reality is that suspending them doesn't do any good. They just come back and screw up again. Mrs. Teller said that these three people had never screwed up before and had never been suspended before, so how Mrs. Magee could know how they'd be after a suspension was beyond her. Mrs. Magee said she knew from long experience that some people can cut it and some can't, and that that's just the way it is!

I said it sounded like they wanted the same thing—better child care practices by houseparents—and that they had two different ways to try to achieve that: one possibility was firing houseparents when they foul up, another possibility was suspending them; and that maybe there were other possibilities as well, like training all three shifts in crisis work, or even having regular re-training sessions.

Proposing Superordinate Goals

A superordinate goal is one which takes precedence over other goals either because it is larger, or more important, or more urgent, or more basic than those other goals. Secondly, it is a goal to which all the various parties whose other goals may conflict with each other can still subscribe. On a national scale, the superordinate goal of national security takes precedence over partisan interests. In the social welfare arena, the superordinate goal of obtaining the funds to continue operating a particular social service program takes precedence over in-house conflict regarding distribution of staff. A direct practice example is provided by the clinician who is adamantly against labeling, yet uses DSM-III-R codes to enable her clients to qualify for health insurance benefits.

The superordinate goal, because of its commanding nature and broad-based appeal can often unite people who are in conflict over other matters and can even reduce pre-existing friction and antagonism. In fact, the superordinate goal seems to be the single most significant factor in dispelling hostility and promoting interpersonal harmony.[3]

In the following example, a social worker at a settlement house helps bridge two neighborhoods by proposing a superordinate goal.

Wilson House serves the Northport and Cedar Hill neighborhoods, both of which have mostly single-parent families living on AFDC and food stamps. But even though they have lots of similar needs and problems, they don't mix. When we offered aerobics classes and card parties at the same time as children's activities so the mothers could have some adult time with each other, if a few Northport women showed up, when a Cedar Hill woman would look in, she'd just leave. And vice versa. They did let their kids mix at our place (like at school, I guess), but not elsewhere. When I asked some of them why, they just said they want to be with their own friends. There certainly wasn't any obvious animosity, but they clearly refused to get together.

So when we decided to start a badly needed free lunch program for children and teens, I told several Northport mothers about it and said they'd have to volunteer, along with Cedar Hill mothers, to shop, cook, serve, and clean up six days a week — ten mothers a day, five from each neighborhood, so kids from both neighborhoods would feel comfortable. I said there are a lot of hungry kids in both areas because food stamps don't stretch too far. I told Cedar Hill mothers the same thing. By the end of the week, the sign-up sheets for each day were full — five from each neighborhood. When the program started two weeks later, the volunteers were kind of formal and kept to themselves, though they worked with each other and the program ran pretty smoothly. By the end of the third week, though, there was laughter in the kitchen, and by mid-summer, some of the volunteers from both neighborhoods were coming an hour earlier for aerobics.

Notes

PREFACE

1. Ruth R. Middleman, *The Non-Verbal Method in Working with Groups* (New York: Association Press, 1968).

2. Jurgen Ruesch and Weldon Keyes, *Non-Verbal Communication* (Berkeley: University of California Press, 1956); Jurgen Ruesch, "Nonverbal Language and Therapy" in Alfred G. Smith, ed., *Communication and Culture* (New York: Holt, Rinehart, and Winston, 1966), pp. 209–13; Milton M. Berger, "Nonverbal Communication in Group Psychotherapy," *International Journal of Group Psychotherapy* (April 1958) 8(2):161–78; Randall Harrison, "Nonverbal Communication: Exploration Into Time, Space, Action, and Object," in James H. Campbell and Hal W. Hepler, eds., *Dimensions in Communication* (Belmont, Calif.: Wadsworth, 1965), pp. 256–71.

3. "Engaging in the Medium of the Other" and "Proposing a Medium Presumably Congenial to the Other," in chapter 3, "Skills for Setting the Stage."

4. Ruth R. Middleman, "An Experimental Field Study of the Impact of Nonverbal Communication of Affect on Children from Two Socio-Economic Backgrounds," Ed.D. dissertation, Temple University, 1971; Gale Goldberg, "Effects of Nonverbal Teacher Behavior on Student Performance," Ed.D. dissertation, Temple University, 1972.

5. Ruth R. Middleman, "The Impact of Nonverbal Communication Upon Black and White Elementary School Children," 3d National Association of Social Workers Professional Symposium, New Orleans, 1972; Gale Goldberg and Cathleen Mayerberg, "Emotional Reactions of Students to Nonverbal Teacher Behavior," *Journal of Experimental Education* (Fall 1973), 42(1); Gale Goldberg and Cathleen Mayerberg, "Effects of Nonverbal Teacher Behavior on Student Performance," *Child Study Journal* (1975), 5(2):

6. See references to our publications in the endnotes of other chapters.

7. Ruth R. Middleman and Gale Goldberg, *Social Service Delivery: A Structural Approach to Social Work Practice* (New York: Columbia University Press, 1974).

8. Gale Goldberg Wood and Ruth R. Middleman, *The Structural Approach*

to *Direct Practice in Social Work* (New York: Columbia University Press, 1989).

INTRODUCTION

1. Daisetz T. Suzuki, "Introduction" in Eugen Herrigel, *Zen in the Art of Archery* (New York: Vintage, 1971), p. 11.

2. Ruth R. Middleman, "The Myth of the Agency as Partner: Social Work Education," *The Centennial Proceedings: 1973 Social Welfare Forum* (New York: Columbia University Press and National Conference on Social Welfare, 1974), pp. 193–212.

3. Martin Bloom, "Analysis of Research on Educating Social Work Students," *Journal of Education for Social Work* (Fall 1976), 12(3):7.

4. For example, Allen E. Ivey, *Microcounseling* (Springfield, Ill.: Charles C. Thomas, 1971); Gerard Egan, *The Skilled Helper* (Monterey, Calif.: Brooks/Cole, 1975); Gerard Egan, *Interpersonal Living* (Monterey, Calif.: Brooks/Cole, 1976); Egan, *You and Me: The Skills of Communicating and Relating to Others* (Monterey, Calif.: Brooks/Cole, 1977); Steven J. Danish and Allen L. Hauer, *Helping Skills: A Basic Training Program* (New York: Behavioral Publications, 1973); Norman Kagan, *Interpersonal Process Recall* (East Lansing, Mich.: Mason Media, 1975); John W. Loughary and Theresa M. Ripley, *Helping Others Help Themselves: A Guide to Counseling Skills* (New York: McGraw-Hill, 1979).

5. An influential innovation in publishing the teaching components involved in training packages of skills, attitudes, concepts, and other structured experiences was the work of J. William Pfeiffer and John E. Jones of University Associates (San Diego, Calif.). Starting in 1969 and yearly thereafter they published *The Handbook of Structured Experiences for Human Relations Training,* and *Annual Handbook for Group Facilitators,* 1972, 1973, 1974, and yearly.

6. *NASW News* (November 1976) 21(10):5.

7. Bernard Ross and S. K. Kinduka, eds., *Social Work in Practice* (Washington, D.C.: National Association of Social Workers, 1976).

8. Jean Hines (University of Iowa, School of Social Work), letter to directors of social work programs April 24, 1978.

9. Harold Lewis, "The Structure of Professional Skill," in Bernard Ross and S. K. Kinduka, eds., *Social Work in Practice,* p. 10.

10. Laura Epstein, "Task-Centered Treatment After Five Years," in Bernard Ross and S. K. Kinduka, eds., *Social Work in Practice,* pp. 77–91.

11. George Brager and Harry Specht, *Community Organizing* (New York: Columbia University Press, 1973), pp. 284–353.

12. Rosemary C. Sarri, "Skills for Administrative and Policy Roles," in Bernard Ross and S. K. Kinduka, eds., *Social Work in Practice,* pp. 142–53.

13. Ruth R. Middleman and Gale Goldberg, *Social Service Delivery: A Structural Approach to Social Work Practice* (New York: Columbia Univer-

sity Press, 1974), pp. 83–150; Gale Goldberg and Ruth Middleman, *I-View Skills: Interviewing Skills for the Human Services* (Park Forest, Ill.: Outp St Software, 1987).

14. Michael Argyle, *The Psychology of Interpersonal Behavior* (Middlesex, England: Penguin, 1967).

15. Carl R. Rogers, "The Necessary and Sufficient Conditions of Therapeutic Personality Change," *Journal of Consulting Psychology* (1957), 22:95–103.

16. C. G. Truax and Robert E. Carkhuff, *Toward Effective Counseling and Psychotherapy* (Chicago: Aldine, 1967).

17. Sidney A. Fine and Wretha W. Wiley, *An Introduction to Functional Job Analysis* (Kalamazoo, Mich.: Upjohn Institute, 1971).

18. Sidney A. Fine and Wretha W. Wiley, *An Introduction to Functional Job Analysis,* pp. 25–26; 79–80.

19. Helen Kiel, "The Concept of Skill in Social Work Education: A Review of the Literature," *Contemporary Social Work Education.* (1982) 5(1):44–57.

20. Eldon K. Marshall, P. David Kurtz, and associates, *Interpersonal Helping Skills* (San Francisco: Jossey-Bass, 1982), pp. 3–25.

21. Eldon K. Marshall, P. David Kurtz, and associates, *Interpersonal Helping Skills.* Some influential approaches in social work that emphasize skills include the works of Lawrence Shulman, *A Casebook of Social Work with Groups* (New York: Council on Social Work Education, 1968); *The Skills of Helping Individuals and Groups* (Itaska, Ill.: Peacock, 1979); Laura Epstein, *Talking and Listening* (St. Louis: Time Mirror/Mosby, 1985); and *Skills of Supervision and Staff Management* (Itaska, Ill.: Peacock, 1982); Dean H. Hepworth and Jo Ann Larsen, *Direct Social Work Practice: Theory and Skills* (Chicago: Dorsey, 1986). In Frank W. Clark, Morton L. Arkava, and associates, *The Pursuit of Competence in Social Work* (San Francisco: Jossey-Bass, 1979), a rich collection of chapters reflecting ideas about skills, teaching, and assessment can be found.

22. Harold Lewis, "Developing A Program Responsive to New Knowledge and Values," in Edward J. Mullen and James Dumpson, eds., *Evaluation of Social Intervention,* pp. 71–89 (San Francisco: Jossey-Bass, 1972).

23. Scott Briar and Henry Miller, *Problems and Issues in Social Casework* (New York: Columbia University Press, 1971), p. 184.

24. Michael Argyle, *The Psychology of Interpersonal Behavior.*

25. Gilbert Ryle, *The Concept of Mind* (New York: Barnes and Noble, 1949), pp. 25–61.

26. Robert L. Barker, *The Social Work Dictionary* (Silver Spring, Md.: National Association of Social Workers, 1987).

1. PERCEPTION SKILLS

1. For further elaboration, see Ruth R. Middleman, "Role of Perception and Cognition in Change," in Aaron Rosenblatt and Diana Waldfogel, eds.,

Handbook of Clinical Social Work (San Francisco: Jossey-Bass, 1983), pp. 229–51; Paul Chance, "Seeing Is Believing," *Psychology Today*, (January/ February 1989), 23(1/2):26; Gregory Sawin, "Can Expectations Influence Perceptions and Attitudes?" *Et cetera* (Spring 1989), 46(1):70–71; Jerome Bruner, *Actual Minds, Possible Worlds* (Cambridge, Mass.: Harvard University Press, 1986), pp. 46–48.

2. For a full description of diverse cognitive styles, see Samuel Messick and associates, *Individuality in Learning* (San Francisco: Jossey-Bass, 1976).

3. See, for example, Peter L. Berger and Thomas Luckmann, *The Social Construction of Reality* (Garden City, N.Y.: Anchor, 1967); Magorah Maruyama, "Cross-Cultural Perspectives on Social and Community Change," in Edward Seidman, ed., *Handbook of Social Intervention*, pp. 33–47 (Beverly Hills, Calif.: Sage, 1983); Joan Berzoff, "From Separation to Connection: Shifts in Understanding Women's Development," *Affilia* (Spring 1989), 4(1):45–58.

4. Donald M. Wolfe and David A. Kolb, "Career Development, Personal Growth, and Experiential Learning," in David A. Kolb, Irwin M. Rubin, and James M. McIntyre, eds., *Organizational Psychology*, pp. 535–63 (Englewood Cliffs, N.J.: Prentice-Hall, 1979); Peter Reason and John Rowan, eds., *Human Inquiry: A Sourcebook of New Paradigm Research* (New York: John Wiley, 1981).

5. Middleman, "Role of Perception," pp. 230–32.

6. For elaboration on different seeing and thinking, as in differences between work with individuals and with groups, see Gale Goldberg, "Breaking the Thought Barriers: New Frontiers in Social Work with Groups," in Marcos Leiderman, Martin L. Birnbaum, and Barbara Dazzo (eds.), *Roots and New Frontiers in Social Group Work* (New York: Haworth, 1988), pp. 203–16.

7. Middleman, "Role of Perception," p. 237.

8. Ruth R. Middleman and Gale Goldberg, "The Interactional Way of Presenting Generic Social Work Concepts," *Journal of Education for Social Work* (Spring 1972), 8(1):48–57; Ruth R. Middleman and Gale Goldberg, "Visual Teaching," paper presented at Annual Program Meeting of the Council on Social Work Education, Chicago, March 10, 1975. Gale Goldberg and Ruth R. Middleman, "It Might Be a Boa Constrictor Digesting an Elephant: Vision Stretching in Social Work Education," *International Journal of Social Work Education* (1980), 3(1):213–25; Ruth R. Middleman and Gale Goldberg, "Maybe It's a Priest or a Lady with a Hat with a Tree on It, or Is It a Bumblebee? Teaching Group Workers to See," *Social Work with Groups* (Spring 1985), 8(1):3–15, reprinted in Marvin Parnes, ed., *Innovations in Social Group Work: Feedback from Practice to Theory* (New York: Haworth, 1985), pp. 29–41.

9. Martini-Bikini Illusion in Roger Shepard, "The Mental Image," *American Psychologist* (February 1978), 38:125–37.

10. We acknowledge the influence of Gordon's two key emphases in his approach to creativity in problem solving: making the familiar strange and

making the strange familiar. See, William J. J. Gordon, *Synectics* (New York: Harper and Row, 1961).

11. Donald A. Schön, *The Reflective Practitioner: How Professionals Think in Action* (New York: Basic Books, 1983).

12. Gregory Bateson, *Mind and Nature: A Necessary Unity* (New York: Bantam Books, 1980), pp. 90–98.

13. Jerome Bruner, *Actual Minds, Possible Worlds,* p. 10.

14. For further description of group process stages, see James A. Garland, Hubert E. Jones, and Ralph A. Kolody, "A Model for Stages of Development in Social Group Work," in Saul Bernstein, ed., *Explorations in Group Work* (Boston: Milford House, 1973), pp. 12–53.

2. COGNITIVE SKILLS

1. Kenneth Bullmer, in *The Art of Empathy* (New York: Human Sciences Press, 1975), describes empathy as the process by which a person accurately perceives another person's feelings and their meaning.

2. Karl H. Pribram describes the as-if thought process by which we use analogy to stretch beyond the limits of our knowledge in "The Role of Analogy in Trancending Limits in the Brain," *Daedalus* (1980), 109(2):19–38; See, too, Edward De Bono's description of lateral process thinking in *New Think* (New York: Avon, 1971), and his development of Po, in *Po: A Device for Successful Thinking* (New York: Simon and Schuster, 1972).

3. For an interesting discussion of humankind's built-in directive to "jump to conclusions," see Leon N. Cooper, "Source and Limits of Human Intellect," *Daedalus* (1980), 109(2):1–17.

4. See Donald A. Schön, *The Reflective Practitioner: How Professionals Think in Action* (New York: Basic Books, 1983), for a discussion of professions facing these complexities.

5. According to Jerome Bruner, "Much of the process of education consists of being able to distance oneself in some way from what one knows by being able to reflect on one's own knowledge." *Actual Minds, Possible Worlds* (Cambridge, Mass.: Harvard Press, 1986), p. 127.

3. SKILLS FOR SETTING THE STAGE

1. See Erving Goffman, *The Presentation of Self in Everyday Life* (Garden City, N.Y.: Doubleday, 1959).

2. Edward T. Hall, "A System for the Notation of Proxemic Behavior," *American Anthropologist* (1963), 45:1003–26; Hall, *Beyond Culture* (Garden City, N.Y.: Doubleday/Anchor, 1977); Hall, *The Hidden Dimension* (Garden City, N.Y.: Doubleday, 1966).

3. Kenneth B. Little, "Personal Space," *Journal of Experimental Social*

Psychology (1965), 1:37–64; Robert Sommer, *Personal Space: the Behavioral Basis of Design* (Englewood Cliffs, N.J.: Prentice-Hall, 1969).

4. Dale F. Lott and Robert Sommer, "Seating Arrangements and Status," *Journal of Personality and Social Psychology* (1967), 7:90–95.

5. Michael Argyle, *The Psychology of Interpersonal Behavior* (Baltimore: Pelican, 1967), p. 32; Albert E. Scheflen, "Stream and Structure of Communicational Behavior," *Behavioral Studies* (1965), vol. 1.

6. Lott and Sommer, "Seating Arrangements and Status"; Paul Hare and Robert Bales, "Seating Position and Small Group Interaction," *Sociometry* (1963), 26:480–86.

7. Robert K. Myers, "Some Effects of Seating Arrangements in Counseling," Ph.D. diss., University of Florida, Gainsville, 1969.

8. Sommer, *Personal Space.*

9. Hall, "A System for the Notation of Proxemic Behavior," p. 1009.

10. Argyle, *The Psychology of Interpersonal Behavior*, p. 108.

11. Adam Kendon, "Some Functions of Gaze Direction in Social Interaction," *Acta Psychologica* (1967) 26(1):1–47.

12. Hall, "A System for the Notation of Proxemic Behavior."

13. Lott and Sommer, "Seating Arrangements and Status"; Hare and Bales, "Seating Position and Small Group Interaction"; Bernard M. Bass and Stanley Kluback, "Effects of Seating Arrangements on Leaderless Group Discussions, *Journal of Abnormal and Social Psychology* (1952), 724–7; Lloyd T. Howells and Selwyn W. Becker, "Seating Arrangements and Leadership Emergence," *Journal of Abnormal Social Psychology* (1962), 44:148–50.

14. Ruth R. Middleman, *The Non-Verbal Method in Working with Groups* (New York: Association Press, 1968).

15. Albert F. Scheflen, "Human Communication: Behavioral Programs and Their Integration," *Behavioral Science* (1968), 13(1):44–55, and "Non-Language Behavior in Communication" (Paper delivered at New York Chapter of the American Academy of Pediatrics, 1969.

16. Harold Lewis, *The Inner-Directed Professional Question: Knowledge, Values, and Action in Social Work* (New York: Hunter College School of Social Work, 1971), pp. 125–30; and Harold Lewis, *The Intellectual Base of Social Work Practice* (New York: Silberman Fund and Haworth, 1982), pp. 63–75.

17. Lewis discusses the internal professional questions "What am I to do now?" and "How am I to act in this situation?" ibid., p. 8.

18. Gale Goldberg and Ruth R. Middleman, "It Might Be a Boa Constrictor Digesting an Elephant: Vision Stretching in Social Work Education," *International Journal of Social Work Education* (1980), 3(1):213–25.

19. For further discussion of social interaction skills, see Argyle, *The Psychology of Interpersonal Behavior*, pp. 86–96.

20. Reporting one's own feelings is further elaborated in chapter 4.

21. For other concepts related to following the other, see "focused listen-

ing" in Allen E. Ivey, *Microcounseling* (Springfield, Ill.: Charles C. Thomas, 1971), p. 57; also, "active listening," a concept elaborated by Thomas Gordon, *Parent Effectiveness Training: the No-Lose Program for Raising Responsible Children* (New York: Wyden, 1970).

22. See Ivey, *Microcounseling*, 56–67 and 152–53, for a description of the skill "minimal encourages to talk" for further details of these types of cues. The major point of this skill is to show interest and involvement but to allow the client to determine the primary direction of the interview, through use of "um-humm," one-word questions, facial expressions, or repeating one or two words the client just said.

23. Incongruent communication in which the verbal and nonverbal segments of the message convey opposite meanings, the double-bind, is a concept that must be credited to Gregory Bateson and has been discussed extensively in the literature on human communication. In double-bind instances there is no way out if one were to follow both messages. See Jurgen Ruesch, *Communication: the Social Matrix of Society* (New York: Norton, 1951); Paul Watzlawick, Janet Beavin, and Don Jackson, *The Pragmatics of Human Communication* (New York: Norton, 1967).

24. Michael M. Reese and Robert N. Whitman, "Expressive Movements, Warmth, and Verbal Reinforcement," *Journal of Abnormal and Social Psychology* (1962), 44:254–86. For other indicators of positive emotion, see chapter 4.

4. SKILLS FOR DEALING WITH FEELINGS

1. For further discussion of the way "emotion reduces the uptake of cues," see Jerome Bruner, *Actual Minds, Possible Worlds* (Cambridge, Mass.: Harvard University Press, 1986), p. 112.

2. See Robert B. Zajonc's discussion in "Feeling and Thinking," *American Psychologist* (1980), 35(2):151–75.

3. For related material on empathic communication, especially its tendency to give clients tacit permission to discuss their feelings, see Jerry Authier and Kay Gustafson, "Microtraining: Focusing on Specific Skills," in Eldon K. Marshall, P. David Kurtz, and associates, *Interpersonal Helping Skills*, pp. 93–130 (San Francisco: Jossey-Bass, 1982).

4. For theory and research on the "punctuation" function of nonverbal behavior, see Albert E. Scheflen, "The Significance of Posture in Communication Systems," *Psychiatry* (1964) 27:316–31; See also, Albert E. Scheflen, *How Behavior Means* (New York: Jason Aronson, 1974).

5. According to Bruner, *Actual Minds Possible Worlds*, even the history of science is full of metaphors used as crutches to help us up the abstract mountains. And once we get there, we can throw them away.

6. Thomas Keefe discusses other skills for helping people deal with stress in "Stress-Coping Skills," *Social Casework* (1988), 68:8.

5. SKILLS FOR DEALING WITH INFORMATION

1. See the discussion of "open invitation to talk," in Allen E. Ivey, *Microcounseling* (Springfield, Ill.: Charles C. Thomas, 1971).

2. The use of open-ended questions to explore is consistent with Gregory Bateson's statement that "an explorer can never know what he is exploring until it has been explored," *Steps to an Ecology of Mind* (New York: Ballantine Books, 1972), p. xiv.

3. Jerome Bruner would call this an act of "disambiguation," *Actual Minds, Possible Worlds* (Cambridge, Mass.: Harvard University Press, 1986), p. 64.

4. The importance of checking out *conscious* inferences is underscored by Jacob Bronowski's statement that "perception . . . is governed by mechanisms which make our knowledge of the outside world highly inferential. Our sense impressions are themselves constructed by the nervous system in such a way that they automatically carry with them an interpretation of what they see or hear or feel," *The Origins of Knowledge and Imagination* (New Haven, Conn.: Yale University Press, 1979), p. 43.

5. For more on seeing from different points of view, see Roger von Oech, *A Whack on the Side of the Head* (New York: Warner, 1983). See, too, James L. Adams, *Conceptual Blockbusting* (San Francisco: W. H. Freeman, 1974), pp. 22–24.

6. Bruner, *Actual Minds, Possible Worlds,* p. 125, makes the point that giving information empowers by balancing an imbalance.

7. This is akin to "brainstorming," one technique for generating alternatives. For specifics of the technique, see Adams, *Conceptual Blockbusting,* pp. 115–16.

8. For additional uses of summarizing, especially those geared toward influencing clients, see Jerry Authier and Kay Gustafson, "Microtraining: Focusing on Specific Skills", in Eldon K. Marshall, P. David Kurtz, and associates, eds., *Interpersonal Helping Skills,* (San Francisco: Jossey-Bass, 1982), pp. 93–130.

6. ABOUT GROUPS

1. Lynn Videka-Sherman, *Harriet M. Bartlett Effectiveness Project Report to NASW Board of Directors* (Silver Spring, Md.: National Association of Social Workers, 1985).

2. See, for example, Morton A. Lieberman and associates, *Self-Help Groups for Coping with Crisis* (San Francisco: Jossey-Bass, 1979).

3. Lynne B. Rosewater and Lenore E. A. Walker, *Handbook of Feminist Therapy* (New York: Springer, 1985); Claire M. Brody, ed., *Women's Therapy Groups* (New York: Springer, 1987).

4. Ruth R. Middleman and Gale Goldberg, "Social Work Practice with Groups," *Encyclopedia of Social Work*, 18th ed. (New York: Columbia University Press, 1987), pp. 714–49; Gale Goldberg Wood and Ruth R. Middleman,

A Structural Approach to Social Work Practice (New York: Columbia University Press, 1989), chapter 11.

5. Ronald W. Toseland, Joan Palmer-Ganeles, and Dennis Chapman, "Teamwork in Psychiatric Settings," *Social Work* (January–February 1986), 31(1):46–52.

7. CONTINUOUS GROUP SKILLS

1. "Thinking group" is a shorthand for knowing concepts and processes that may be found in any group dynamics text. While the social worker, ideally, should have taken a background course in these group matters, at least a familiarity with some group literature is desirable.

2. Ann Melzer Bergart, "Isolation to Intimacy: Incest Survivors in Group Therapy," *Social Casework* (1986), 67(5):272–73. For reasons of clarity, "the author" in Bergart's text was changed to "I" or "me."

3. Susan Hartman, "A Self-Help Group for Women in Abusive Relationships," *Social Work with Groups* (1983), 6(4):136–38.

4. All texts that deal with group processes and dynamics place high priority on cohesiveness. It was described as a key factor in the effectiveness of groups by Dorwin Cartwright, "On the Nature of Group Cohesiveness," in Dorwin Cartwright and Alvin Zander, eds., *Group Dynamics: Research and Theory,* pp. 91–109 (New York: Harper and Row, 1968); for example, Martin Lakin and Philip R. Costanzo, "The Leader and the Experiential Group," in Cary L. Cooper, ed., *Theories of Group Processes* (New York: Wiley, 1975), pp. 205–34, deal with it first in their discussion of core processes in all groups, educational or therapeutic. Cohesiveness must be achieved and maintained.

8. SKILLS FOR BUILDING GROUPS

1. Norma C. Lang and Joanne Sulman, eds., "Collectivity in Social Group Work: Concept and Practice," *Social Work with Groups* (Winter 1986), vol. 9, issue 4.

2. Nazneen S. Mayadas and Wayne D. Duehn, "Leadership Skills in Treatment Groups," in Eldon K. Marshall, P. David Kurtz, and associates, *Interpersonal Helping Skills* pp. 314–36 (San Francisco: Jossey-Bass, 1982), described and operationalized twelve leadership behaviors for work in groups. Four (reinforcement of group's verbal interaction, reinforcement of individual responses, reinforcement of group importance, and reinforcement of intra-group focus) are especially focused on the concept of groupness.

3. James A. Garland, Hubert E. Jones, and Ralph L. Kolodny, "A Model for Stages of Development in Social Work Groups," in Saul Bernstein, ed., *Explorations in Group Work* (Boston: Boston University School of Social Work, 1965), p. 43.

4. Abraham A. Low, *Mental Health Through Will-Training* (Winnetka,

Ill.: Willett, 1950; "Recovery Rules" (Louisville, Ky.,: Recovery, Inc. of Kentucky, n.d.), photocopied).

5. Toronto Women's Support Group Collective, *Helping Ourselves: A Handbook for Women Starting Groups* (Toronto, Canada: The Women's Press, 1985), p. 131.

9. SKILLS FOR FACILITATING THE WORK OF THE GROUP

1. Mehrabian terms such cues subtle because there are no formal, organized ways to deal with them (dictionaries, agreed-upon coding, rules for syntax and grammar) in contrast to words. That is, these behaviors remain subtle for us, not because they are less powerful than words, not because we know less about their function and usage. For further discussion of "implicit" and "explicit" aspects of language, see Albert Mehrabian, *Nonverbal Communication* (Chicago: Aldine-Atherton, 1972), ch. 1.

2. Jurgen Ruesch and Gregory Bateson, *Communication: the Social Matrix of Society* (New York: Norton, 1951).

3. For further elaboration refer to discussion of "Courtroom" in Eric Berne, *Games People Play* (New York: Grove Press, 1964), pp. 96–98.

4. For a rich source of material focused on gender issues in group work see Beth Glover Reed and Charles D. Garvin, eds., *Group Work with Women/ Groupwork with Men* (New York: Haworth, 1983), especially the skills-focused chapter of Eileen Gambrill and Cheryl A. Richey, "Gender Issues Related to Group Social Skills Training," pp. 51–66.

5. Empowerment through participation in groups is highlighted in Judith A. B. Lee, ed., *Group Work with the Poor and Oppressed* (New York: Haworth, 1988).

6. For added examination of aspects of consensus seeking and conflict in groups, see Stanley E. Jones, Dean C. Barnlund, and Franklyn S. Haiman, *The Dynamics of Discussion: Communication in Small Groups* (New York: Harper and Row, 1980), pp. 146–51.

7. Ibid., pp. 134–39, elaborates conflicts and differences in groups.

8. Irving L. Janis, *Victims of Groupthink* (Boston: Houghton Mifflin, 1972).

10. SKILLS FOR NON-TALKING GROUPS AND NON-TALKING TIMES WITH GROUPS

1. See, for example, George Spivak and Myrna Shure, *Social Adjustment of Young Children* (San Francisco: Jossey-Bass, 1974).

2. For example, Maury Smith, *A Practical Guide to Value Clarification* (La Jolla, Calif.: University Associates, 1977); J. William Pfeiffer and John E. Jones, the numerous handbooks of *Structured Experiences for Human Relations Training,* yearly since 1969; and Jones and Pfeiffer, *Annual Handbook for Group Facilitators,* yearly since 1972, University Associates, La Jolla, Calif.: Louise Yolton Eberhardt, *Working with Women's Groups* (Duluth,

Minn.: Whole Person Press, 1987); Roger Karsk and Bill Thomas, *Working with Men's Groups* (Duluth, Minn.: Whole Person Press, 1986).

3. Ruth R. Middleman, "The Use of Program in Group Work: Review and Update," *Social Work with Groups* (1980), 3(3):5–14.

4. See Ruth R. Middleman, *The Non-Verbal Method in Working with Groups* (New York: Association Press, 1968), for a fuller discussion of pursuing social group work purposes through activities, especially pp. 174–258, "Eighty Case Studies—Anecdotal Accounts of the Use of Non-Verbal Content with a Special Consideration of the Purpose of the Activity."

5. Ruth R. Middleman, "The Pursuit of Competence through Involvement in Structured Groups," in Anthony Mallucio, ed., *Building Competence in Clients* (New York: Free Press, 1981), pp. 185–210.

6. See Donald F. Fausel's interview with Elizabeth McGonagle, *Journal of Independent Social Work* (Summer 1988), vol. 2, issue 4.

11. SKILLS FOR DEALING WITH BARRIERS

1. For related material, see Laura Epstein, *Talking and Listening* (St. Louis: Times Mirror/Mosby, 1985), pp. 15–16.

2. For a fuller discussion, see Merton M. Gill, *Analysis of Transference* (New York: International Universities Press, 1982), vol. 1.

3. James L. Adams describes taboos as conceptual blocks in *Conceptual Blockbusting* (San Francisco: W. H. Freeman, 1974).

4. For specifics, see Diane de Anda, "Bicultural Socialization: Factors Affecting the Minority Experience", *Social Work* (1984), 29(2):101–7; see, also, H. C. Triandis, ed., *Variations in Black and White Perceptions of the Social Environment* (Urbana: University of Illinois Press, 1976).

12. SKILLS FOR COPING WITH CONFLICT

1. For descriptions of other ways to forestall and sidestep conflict, see Herb Bisno, *Managing Conflict* (Newbury Park, Calif.: Sage, 1988).

2. For further discussion of managing conflicts and disagreements, see Elam Nunnally and Caryl Moy, *Communication Basics for Human Service Professionals* (Newbury Park, Calif.: Sage, 1989).

3. Musafer Sharif, "Superordinate Goals in the Reduction of Intergroup Conflict," *American Journal of Sociology* (1958), 63:349–56.

Index